60 Promises to
Pray Over
Your
Children

DaySpring

LIVE YOUR FAITH

60 Promises to
Pray Over
Your
Children

Contents

A Message to Parents

As a Christian, you undoubtedly understand the power of prayer. And as a parent, you know the importance of praying for your child. This book provides sixty prayers that address topics that are vitally important to you and your youngster. The text also contains timely quotations from notable Christians and timeless promises from God's holy Word.

God has made many promises to you *and* to your child. The Lord's promises are eternal and unchanging, but in today's fast-paced world, circumstances can be so demanding and situations so confusing that it's easy to forget God's blessings and His mercy. This book is intended to remind you of the joy and the abundance that the Lord offers to all His children, including yours.

As a concerned parent living in the twenty-first century, you already know that your child inhabits a world that's brimming with temptations and distractions. Despite your best efforts, you simply can't protect your youngster from every spiritual trap and every physical danger. That's where God comes in. Nothing is impossible for Him. When you ask for His help and His guidance, He'll respond in miraculous ways.

So take heart and have faith. When you pray for your children, you're fulfilling a profound parental duty. And remember this: There's absolutely no challenge—not even the critically important challenge of caring for your kids—that you and God, working together, can't handle.

1

Abundance

The Promise of Abundance

My cup runs over. Surely goodness and mercy
shall follow me all the days of my life;
and I will dwell in the house of the LORD forever.

PSALM 23:5–6 NKJV

I thank You, dear Lord, for Your abundance. You have blessed my family in so many ways. I pray that my children will receive Your abundance. And I pray that they will be grateful for Your blessings.

Today, Father, I pray that my family will claim the joy that comes from the knowledge that Your love is eternal. We will praise You, Lord, for Your grace.

I am grateful for the abundant life that Jesus promised. Grant me the wisdom to claim Christ's blessings and to share them with my children. And lead me, Lord, on Your path today, tomorrow, and every day of my life.

Amen.

More from God's Word

Until now you have asked for nothing
in My name. Ask and you will receive,
that your joy may be complete.

JOHN 16:24 HCSB

And God is able to make all grace abound to you,
so that always having all sufficiency in everything,
you may have an abundance for every good deed.

II CORINTHIANS 9:8 NASB

Young men and young women, old men and children.
Let them all praise the name of the LORD.
For his name is very great; his glory towers
over the earth and heaven! He has made
his people strong, honoring his faithful ones. . . .

PSALM 148:12–14 NLT

May Yahweh bless you and protect you; may Yahweh
make His face shine on you and be gracious to you.

NUMBERS 6:24–25 HCSB

About Abundance

*God loves you and wants you to experience
peace and life—abundant and eternal.*

BILLY GRAHAM

*The man who lives without Jesus is the poorest
of the poor, whereas no one is so rich
as the man who lives in His grace.*

THOMAS À KEMPIS

*God is the giver, and we are the receivers.
And His richest gifts are bestowed not upon
those who do the greatest things, but upon those
who accept His abundance and His grace.*

HANNAH WHITALL SMITH

*We honor God by asking for great things when
they are a part of His promise. We dishonor Him
and cheat ourselves when we ask for molehills
where He has promised mountains.*

VANCE HAVNER

2

Acceptance

Accepting God's Sovereignty

Be of good courage, and let us be strong
for our people and for the cities of our God.
And may the LORD do what is good in His sight.

I CHRONICLES 19:13 NKJV

Dear Lord, Your plans are perfect. Even when I do not understand the reason that things happen, I will trust You. And I pray that my children will learn to trust You in every season of life.

I pray that my children will focus on their blessings, not their disappointments. And I pray that they can learn to accept whatever life brings without ever losing faith in You.

This world can be a troubling place. And sometimes things happen that we simply cannot understand. But You understand. In whatever circumstances we find ourselves, let us trust Your perfect plan and accept Your perfect love.

Amen.

More from God's Word

Everything God made is good, and nothing
should be refused if it is accepted with thanks.

I TIMOTHY 4:4 NCV

He is the LORD. He will do what He thinks is good.

I SAMUEL 3:18 HCSB

Trust in the LORD with all your heart
and lean not on your own understanding.

PROVERBS 3:5 NIV

For Yahweh is good, and His love is eternal;
His faithfulness endures through all generations.

PSALM 100:5 HCSB

For now we see in a mirror, dimly,
but then face to face. Now I know in part,
but then I shall know just as I also am known.

I CORINTHIANS 13:12 NKJV

About Acceptance

*Christians who are strong in the faith grow as they
accept whatever God allows to enter their lives.*

BILLY GRAHAM

*God, give us the grace to accept with serenity
the things that cannot be changed, the courage
to change the things that should be changed,
and the wisdom to distinguish the one from the other.*

REINHOLD NIEBUHR

Subdue your heart to match your circumstances.

JONI EARECKSON TADA

*Loving Him means the thankful acceptance
of all things that His love has appointed.*

ELISABETH ELLIOT

*Should we accept only good things from
the hand of God and never anything bad?*

JOB 2:10 NLT

3

Adversity

He Promises to Protect and Heal Us

I called to the LORD in my distress; I called to my God. From His temple He heard my voice. . . .

II SAMUEL 22:7 HCSB

Dear Lord, I pray that You will give my children the strength to meet the inevitable challenges and hardships of life. When my children are fearful, give them courage. When they are discouraged, give them hope. When they are worried, give them faith in the future and faith in You.

I pray that my children will treat their disappointments as opportunities to trust You more. You are always with them, Father, and no problem is too big for You. I pray that they focus on Your love and Your protection, now and forever.

Amen.

More from God's Word

The LORD is my rock, my fortress, and my deliverer,
my God, my mountain where I seek refuge.
My shield, the horn of my salvation,
my stronghold, my refuge, and my Savior. . . .

II SAMUEL 22:2–3 HCSB

God blesses the people who patiently endure testing.
Afterward they will receive the crown of life
that God has promised to those who love him.

JAMES 1:12 NLT

My brethren, count it all joy when you fall into various
trials, knowing that the testing of your faith produces
patience. But let patience have its perfect work, that
you may be perfect and complete, lacking nothing.

JAMES 1:2–4 NKJV

He heals the brokenhearted and binds up their wounds.

PSALM 147:3 HCSB

The LORD is my shepherd; I shall not want.

PSALM 23:1 KJV

About Adversity

*Often God has to shut a door in our face
so that he can subsequently open the door
through which he wants us to go.*

CATHERINE MARSHALL

*When a train goes through a tunnel and it gets dark,
you don't throw away your ticket and jump off.
You sit still and trust the engineer.*

CORRIE TEN BOOM

God will make obstacles serve His purpose.

LETTIE COWMAN

*God is in control. He may not take away trials or make
detours for us, but He strengthens us through them.*

BILLY GRAHAM

*We are hard-pressed on every side, yet not crushed;
we are perplexed, but not in despair.*

II CORINTHIANS 4:8 NKJV

4

Asking God

He Wants Us to Ask

*Ask, and it shall be given to you; seek,
and you shall find; knock, and it shall
be opened to you. For every one who
asks receives, and he who seeks finds,
and to him who knocks it shall be opened.*

MATTHEW 7:7–8 NASB

Dear Lord, I pray that my children will learn to ask You for the things they need. You are always listening, Father. I pray that they will talk to You often.

You know what my children want, Lord, but more importantly, You know what they need.

Your love endures forever. Protect my children, Father. When they have questions, concerns, or fears, I pray that they will turn to You. And I pray that they will trust Your answers today, tomorrow, and forever.

Amen.

More from God's Word

Until now you have asked for nothing in My name.
Ask and you will receive, that your joy may be complete.

JOHN 16:24 HCSB

Do not be anxious about anything,
but in everything, by prayer and petition,
with thanksgiving, present your requests to God.

PHILIPPIANS 4:6 NIV

Your Father knows the things
you have need of before you ask Him.

MATTHEW 6:8 NKJV

The effective prayer of a righteous man
can accomplish much.

JAMES 5:16 NASB

You did not choose me, but I chose you
and appointed you to go and bear fruit—
fruit that will last—as so that whatever
you ask in my name the Father will give you.

JOHN 15:16 NIV

About Asking God

*It's important that you keep asking God
to show you what He wants you to do.
If you don't ask, you won't know.*

STORMIE OMARTIAN

*When you ask God to do something,
don't ask timidly; put your whole heart into it.*

MARIE T. FREEMAN

*God insists that we ask, not because He needs
to know our situation, but because
we need the spiritual discipline of asking.*

CATHERINE MARSHALL

You pay God a compliment by asking great things of Him.

SAINT TERESA OF ÁVILA

*Now this is the confidence we have before Him:
Whenever we ask anything according to His will,
He hears us. And if we know that He hears whatever we
ask, we know that we have what we have asked Him for.*

I JOHN 5:14–15 HCSB

5

Balance

The Promise of Balance, Contentment, and Peace

Come unto me, all ye that labour and are heavy laden, and I will give you rest.

MATTHEW 11:28 KJV

Dear Lord, I pray that my children will discover the contentment and peace that only You can offer. The world promises its own version of peace, but the contentment that the world offers is deceptive and fleeting.

Let Your priorities be their priorities; let their plans be Your plans; let Your will be their will. Let my children find balance, contentment, and peace through You.

When we trust in the things of this earth, we will be disappointed. But when we put our faith in You, we are secure. Let us place our hopes and our trust in Your infinite wisdom and Your boundless love.

Amen.

More from God's Word

Abundant peace belongs to those who love
Your instruction; nothing makes them stumble.

PSALM 119:165 HCSB

Don't burn out; keep yourselves fueled and aflame.
Be alert servants of the Master, cheerfully expectant.
Don't quit in hard times; pray all the harder. . . .

ROMANS 12:11–12 MSG

But godliness with contentment is a great gain.

I TIMOTHY 6:6 HCSB

Careful planning puts you ahead in the long run;
hurry and scurry puts you further behind.

PROVERBS 21:5 MSG

But those who wait on the LORD
Shall renew their strength;
They shall mount up with wings like eagles,
They shall run and not be weary,
They shall walk and not faint.

ISAIAH 40:31 NKJV

About a Balanced Life

*The only way to keep your balance is to fix
your eyes on the One who never changes.
If you gaze too long at your circumstances,
you will become dizzy and confused.*

SARAH YOUNG

*Reading news without reading the Bible
will inevitably lead to an unbalanced life,
an anxious spirit, a worried and depressed soul.*

BILL BRIGHT

*Beware of having so much to do that you
really do nothing at all because
you do not wait upon God to do it right.*

C. H. SPURGEON

*I leave you peace; my peace I give you.
I do not give it to you as the world does.
So don't let your hearts be troubled or afraid.*

JOHN 14:27 NCV

6

Celebration

Celebrating His Gifts

Rejoice always, pray without ceasing,
in everything give thanks; for this is the will of God
in Christ Jesus for you.

I Thessalonians 5:16–18 NKJV

Dear Lord, I pray that my children will celebrate life. I pray that they will rejoice in the tasks You have given them.

You have given our family so many blessings, Father, countless reasons to rejoice and be grateful. We thank You for Your provision and for Your love.

To serve as an example to my children, I will strive to be a joyful Christian, Lord, and I will share my joy with all those who cross my path. You have given me so many reasons to celebrate, and I will rejoice today and every day.

Amen.

More from God's Word

A happy heart is like a continual feast.

PROVERBS 15:15 NCV

This is the day which the LORD has made;
let us rejoice and be glad in it.

PSALM 118:24 NASB

Weeping may stay for the night,
but rejoicing comes in the morning.

PSALM 30:5 NIV

I delight greatly in the LORD;
my soul rejoices in my God.

ISAIAH 61:10 NIV

I came that they may have life,
and have it abundantly.

JOHN 10:10 NASB

About Celebration

Every day we live is a priceless gift of God,
loaded with possibilities to learn something new,
to gain fresh insights.

DALE EVANS ROGERS

Instead of living a black-and-white existence,
we'll be released into a Technicolor world
of vibrancy and emotion when we more accurately
reflect His nature to the world around us.

BILL HYBELS

There is not one blade of grass, there is no color
in this world that is not intended to make us rejoice.

JOHN CALVIN

All our life is celebration to us. We are convinced,
in fact, that God is always everywhere.

SAINT CLEMENT OF ALEXANDRIA

Rejoice in the Lord always. Again I will say, rejoice!

PHILIPPIANS 4:4 NKJV

7

Character

The Importance of Character

He stores up success for the upright;
He is a shield for those who live with integrity.

PROVERBS 2:7 HCSB

Dear Lord, You have promised that You are a shield for those who live righteously. I pray that my children will be Your honest and faithful servants.

The Bible instructs all people to walk in honesty and in truth. You have promised that when we seek Your truth, You will guide us. And You have promised that Your truth will set us free.

Give my children the courage to speak honestly and behave honorably. Let them discover Your truth, and let them walk righteously with You today, tomorrow, and every day of their lives.

Amen.

More from God's Word

The integrity of the upright guides them,
but the perversity of the treacherous destroys them.

PROVERBS 11:3 HCSB

The godly are directed by their honesty.

PROVERBS 11:5 NLT

The godly walk with integrity;
blessed are their children who follow them.

PROVERBS 20:7 NLT

Let integrity and uprightness preserve me,
For I wait for You.

PSALM 25:21 NKJV

About Character

True greatness is not measured by the headlines
or wealth. The inner character of a person
is the true measure of lasting greatness.

BILLY GRAHAM

What happens outwardly in your life is not
as important as what happens inside you.
Your circumstances are temporary,
but your character will last forever.

RICK WARREN

God is interested in developing your character.
At times He lets you proceed, but He will never
let you go too far without discipline to bring you back.

HENRY BLACKABY

Character is what you are in the dark.

D. L. MOODY

Whoever walks in integrity walks securely,
but whoever takes crooked paths will be found out.

PROVERBS 10:9 NIV

8

Contentment

He Offers Us Contentment

Let your conduct be without covetousness; be content with such things as you have. For He Himself has said, "I will never leave you nor forsake you."

HEBREWS 13:5 NKJV

Dear Lord, I pray that my children will find contentment and peace through You. Help them to trust Your Word, to follow Your commandments, and to seek Your guidance. And protect them, Father, from the distractions and temptations that are woven so tightly into the fabric of everyday life.

This world makes promises that it cannot keep. The world promotes its own version of success, and those who trust in the world's promises are inevitably disappointed. But Your promises are true, and those who seek Your peace are inevitably fulfilled.

Genuine peace is found, not in the world, but in You, Father. I pray that my children will trust You always. And I pray that they will discover the only peace that really matters: Your peace.

Amen.

More from God's Word

But godliness with contentment is a great gain.

*Make sure that your character is free from
the love of money, being content with what you have;
for He Himself has said, "I will never desert you,
nor will I ever forsake you."*

*A tranquil heart is life to the body,
but jealousy is rottenness to the bones.*

*Come unto me,
all ye that labour and are heavy laden,
and I will give you rest.*

*The peace of God, which passeth all understanding,
shall keep your hearts and minds through Christ Jesus.*

About Contentment

*Contentment has an internal quietness of heart
that gladly submits to God in all circumstances.*

JONI EARECKSON TADA

*Nobody who gets enough food and clothing
in a world where most people are hungry
and cold has any business to talk about "misery."*

C. S. LEWIS

*No matter what you're facing, embrace life in trust
and contentment based on your faith in Jesus.*

ELIZABETH GEORGE

*When you truly know God, you have energy to serve
him, boldness to share him, and contentment in him.*

J. I. PACKER

I have learned in whatever state I am, to be content.

PHILIPPIANS 4:11 NKJV

9

Courage

He Gives Us Courage

*Be of good courage, and he shall strengthen
your heart, all ye that hope in the LORD.*

PSALM 31:24 KJV

Dear Lord, I pray that my children will turn to You for the courage they need to live righteously and well. I ask that You give them the wisdom to know right from wrong and the strength to do what they know to be right.

Sometimes, Father, we all face difficulties that almost overwhelm us, and we are tempted to give up hope. But You are always with us, Lord, always ready to guide us and protect us. So we can take comfort in the knowledge that You are our Shepherd, today and forever.

This is your day, Lord. You have made it, and You have given it to us as a priceless gift. As a parent, I ask for Your guidance. As for my children, I ask that You lead them on the proper path—Your path—and that You give them the courage to do the right thing, even when it's hard.

Amen.

More from God's Word

Be on guard. Stand firm in the faith.
Be courageous. Be strong.

I Corinthians 16:13 NLT

For God has not given us
a spirit of fearfulness,
but one of power, love,
and sound judgment.

II Timothy 1:7 HCSB

I can do all things through
Him who strengthens me.

Philippians 4:13 NASB

But He said to them,
"It is I; do not be afraid."

John 6:20 NKJV

Behold, God is my salvation;
I will trust, and not be afraid. . . .

Isaiah 12:2 KJV

About Courage

Courage is not simply one of the virtues,
but the form of every virtue at the testing point.

C. S. Lewis

He who faces no calamity will need no courage.
Mysterious though it is, the characteristics
in human nature which we love best grow
in a soil with a strong mixture of troubles.

Harry Emerson Fosdick

Action springs not from thought,
but from a readiness for responsibility.

Dietrich Bonhoeffer

In my experience, God rarely makes our fear disappear.
Instead, he asks us to be strong and take courage.

Bruce Wilkinson

Be strong and courageous, and do the work.
Do not be afraid or discouraged,
for the Lord God, my God, is with you.

I Chronicles 28:20 NIV

10

Daily Devotional

The Promise of Daily Bread

Thy word is a lamp unto my feet,
and a light unto my path.

PSALM 119:105 KJV

Dear Lord, I pray that my children will study Your Word. I pray that they will make the time and take the time to delve deeply into the wisdom and the promises that they find there. And I pray that they will learn to love Your Word.

Heavenly Father, You've given us the Holy Bible, Your book of instructions for life here on earth and for life together with You forever in heaven. I pray that my children will learn to use the Bible as their guide. I pray that they will study it and meditate upon its truth. And I pray that they will listen to Your voice as You speak to them during the quiet moments they spend with You.

Amen.

More from God's Word

It is good to give thanks to the Lord,
And to sing praises to Your name, O Most High.

PSALM 92:1 NKJV

Heaven and earth will pass away,
but My words will never pass away.

MATTHEW 24:35 HCSB

Early the next morning, while it was still dark,
Jesus woke and left the house.
He went to a lonely place, where he prayed.

MARK 1:35 NCV

Your words were found, and I ate them, and Your word
was to me the joy and rejoicing of my heart;
for I am called by Your name, O LORD God of hosts.

JEREMIAH 15:16 NKJV

But grow in the grace and knowledge of our Lord
and Savior Jesus Christ. To Him be the glory
both now and to the day of eternity.

II PETER 3:18 HCSB

About Daily Devotionals

*Make it the first morning business of your life
to understand some part of the Bible clearly,
and make it your daily business to obey it.*

JOHN RUSKIN

Prayer time must be kept up as duly as mealtime.

MATTHEW HENRY

*I believe the reason so many are failing today
is that they have not disciplined themselves
to read God's Word consistently, day in and day out,
and to apply it to every situation in life.*

KAY ARTHUR

*Begin each day with God.
It will change your priorities.*

ELIZABETH GEORGE

*Morning by morning he wakens me and opens
my understanding to his will. The Sovereign LORD
has spoken to me, and I have listened.*

ISAIAH 50:4–5 NLT

11

Encouragement

The Power of Encouragement

Now we exhort you, brethren,
warn those who are unruly, comfort the fainthearted,
uphold the weak, be patient with all.

I THESSALONIANS 5:14 NKJV

Dear Lord, I pray that my children will be helpful, hopeful, encouraging Christians. I pray that they will be quick to praise others and equally quick to share Your message of hope with the world.

This world can be a discouraging place, where so many people have lost their enthusiasm for life. I pray that my children can lift others up with kind words, good deeds, and heartfelt prayers.

You have blessed my family, Father, in so many ways. Now I ask that You use us to be a blessing to others.

Amen.

More from God's Word

Let us think about each other and help each other
to show love and do good deeds.

HEBREWS 10:24 ICB

So encourage each other and give each other strength,
just as you are doing now.

I THESSALONIANS 5:11 NCV

When you talk, do not say harmful things,
but say what people need—words that will help
others become stronger. Then what you say
will do good to those who listen to you.

EPHESIANS 4:29 NCV

Therefore, since we are surrounded by such a huge
crowd of witnesses to the life of faith, let us strip off
every weight that slows us down, especially
the sin that so easily trips us up. And let us run
with endurance the race God has set before us.

HEBREWS 12:1 NLT

About Encouragement

Discouraged people don't need critics.
They hurt enough already. What they need
is encouragement. They need a refuge,
a willing, caring, available someone.

CHARLES SWINDOLL

Correction does much, but encouragement
does more. Encouragement after censure
is as the sun after a shower.

JOHANN WOLFGANG VON GOETHE

Don't forget that a single sentence, spoken at the right
moment, can change somebody's whole perspective on
life. A little encouragement can go a long, long way.

MARIE T. FREEMAN

But encourage each other daily,
while it is still called today, so that none of you
is hardened by sin's deception.

HEBREWS 3:13 HCSB

12

Eternal Life

The Promise of Eternal Life

*I assure you: Anyone who hears My word and believes
Him who sent Me has eternal life and will not come
under judgment but has passed from death to life.*

JOHN 5:24 HCSB

Heavenly Father, You have offered me the gift of eternal
life through Your Son, and I have accepted Your gift
with joy in my heart and praise on my lips. Now I pray
that my children will accept Your Son as their Savior.

Jesus made the ultimate sacrifice on the cross. He
gave His earthly life so that we might live with Him in
heaven. Let us share the good news with all those who
need Christ's healing touch.

Dear Lord, keep the hope of heaven fresh in our
hearts today and every day.

Amen.

More from God's Word

For the wages of sin is death, but the gift of God
is eternal life in Christ Jesus our Lord.

ROMANS 6:23 NIV

I have written these things to you who believe
in the name of the Son of God, so that you
may know that you have eternal life.

I JOHN 5:13 HCSB

The world and its desires pass away,
but the man who does the will of God lives forever.

I JOHN 2:17 NIV

The last enemy that will be destroyed is death.

I CORINTHIANS 15:26 NKJV

And God raised us up with Christ and seated us
with him in the heavenly realms in Christ Jesus,
in order that in the coming ages he might show
the incomparable riches of his grace,
expressed in his kindness to us in Christ Jesus.

EPHESIANS 2:6–7 NIV

About Eternal Life

Death is not the end of life;
it is only the gateway to eternity.

Billy Graham

When ten thousand times ten thousand times ten thousand
years have passed, eternity will have just begun.

Billy Sunday

Death is not a journeying into an unknown land.
It is a voyage home. We are not going
to a strange country but to our Father's house,
and among our kith and kin.

John Ruskin

Everything that is joined to the immortal Head
will share His immortality.

C. S. Lewis

For God so loved the world, that he gave
his only begotten Son, that whosoever believeth
in him should not perish, but have everlasting life.

John 3:16 KJV

13

Fear

Freedom from Fear

Even though I walk through darkest valley,
I will fear no evil, for you are with me;
your rod and your staff, they comfort me.

PSALM 23:4 NIV

Dear Lord, I pray that You will deliver my children from the shackles of fear. You have promised that even when they walk through the valley of the shadow of death, You are with them. Let them trust Your promises.

Thank You, Father, for Your perfect love, a love that casts out fear and gives me the courage to meet the challenges of this world.

When my children are weary, Lord, give them strength. Give them the confidence, Father, to face the challenges of this day as they gain courage from You. With You as their Protector, they have nothing to fear.

Amen.

More from God's Word

But He said to them, "It is I; do not be afraid."

JOHN 6:20 NKJV

Fear not, for I am with you; Be not dismayed,
for I am your God. I will strengthen you,
Yes, I will help you, I will uphold you
with My righteous right hand.

ISAIAH 41:10 NKJV

The LORD is my light and my salvation—
whom should I fear? The LORD is the stronghold
of my life—of whom should I be afraid?

PSALM 27:1 HCSB

Immediately Jesus spoke to them.
"Have courage! It is I. Don't be afraid."

MATTHEW 14:27 HCSB

Be not afraid, only believe.

MARK 5:36 KJV

About Freedom from Fear

*The presence of fear does not mean
you have no faith. Fear visits everyone.
But make your fear a visitor and not a resident.*

MAX LUCADO

*God shields us from most of the things we fear,
but when He chooses not to shield us,
He unfailingly allots grace in the measure needed.*

ELISABETH ELLIOT

*The Lord Jesus by His Holy Spirit is with me,
and the knowledge of His presence dispels
the darkness and allays any fears.*

BILL BRIGHT

*The presence of hope in the invincible
sovereignty of God drives out fear.*

JOHN PIPER

*Peace I leave with you; My peace I give to you;
not as the world gives do I give to you. Do not let
your heart be troubled, nor let it be fearful.*

JOHN 14:27 NASB

14

Focus

The Power of Focus

*One thing I do, forgetting those things which
are behind and reaching forward to those things which
are ahead, I press toward the goal for the prize
of the upward call of God in Christ Jesus.*

PHILIPPIANS 3:13–14 NKJV

Dear Lord, this world is filled with so many distractions and temptations. Everywhere they turn, my children are faced with opportunities to stray far from Your path. I pray that they can learn to focus on Your calling by making Your priorities their priorities.

I know that You have a perfect plan for my children, Father. If they trust in You, the future is eternally bright for them. So I pray that they seek Your will for their lives and become worthy disciples of Your Son. Help them face each day with a spirit of optimism and thanksgiving. And let them focus their thoughts on You and Your incomparable gifts.

Amen.

More from God's Word

But seek first the kingdom of God and His righteousness,
and all these things will be provided for you.

MATTHEW 6:33 HCSB

Patient endurance is what you need now,
so you will continue to do God's will.
Then you will receive all that he has promised.

HEBREWS 10:36 NLT

Trust in the LORD with all your heart, and do not rely
on your own understanding; think about Him in all
your ways, and He will guide you on the right paths.

PROVERBS 3:5–6 HCSB

Let us lay aside every weight, and the sin
which so easily ensnares us, and let us run
with endurance the race that is set before us.

HEBREWS 12:1 NKJV

I will instruct you and show you the way to go;
with My eye on you, I will give counsel.

PSALM 32:8 HCSB

About Focus

Let's face it. None of us can do a thousand things to the glory of God. And, in our own vain attempt to do so, we stand the risk of forfeiting a precious thing.

BETH MOORE

No horse gets anywhere until he is harnessed. No stream or gas drives anything until it is confined. No life ever grows great until it is focused, dedicated, disciplined.

HARRY EMERSON FOSDICK

It is our best work that God wants, not the dregs of our exhaustion. I think he must prefer quality to quantity.

GEORGE MACDONALD

Give me a person who says, "This one thing I do," and not "These fifty things I dabble in."

D. L. MOODY

Let your eyes look forward; fix your gaze straight ahead.

PROVERBS 4:25 HCSB

15

Fulfillment

He Offers Fulfillment

*I have spoken these things to you so that My joy
may be in you and your joy may be complete.*

John 15:11 HCSB

Dear Lord, I pray that my children will find meaning,
joy, and fulfillment through You. I know that if my
children seek to please You, Father, they will be blessed.
But if they stray from Your path—if they are deceived
by the enemy or caught up in the distractions that
surround them—they will suffer. So I pray that they
will be obedient and faithful to You.

You have given my children so many blessings,
Lord. Let them celebrate Your gifts. Make them joyful
Christians and worthy examples to their friends, to our
family, and to the world.

Amen.

More from God's Word

This is the day the Lord has made;
let us rejoice and be glad in it.

PSALM 118:24 HCSB

A heart at peace gives life to the body,
but envy rots the bones.

PROVERBS 14:30 NIV

I have learned in whatever state I am, to be content.

PHILIPPIANS 4:11 NKJV

But godliness with contentment is a great gain.

I TIMOTHY 6:6 HCSB

The thief's purpose is to steal
and kill and destroy. My purpose is to
give them a rich and satisfying life.

JOHN 10:10 NLT

About Fulfillment

God has laid down spiritual laws which,
if obeyed, bring harmony and fulfillment,
but, if disobeyed, bring discord and disorder.

BILLY GRAHAM

Happiness is not to be found in things,
only in the secret places of the soul.

SAINT THÉRÈSE OF LISIEUX

As we make an offering of our work, we find the truth
of a principle Jesus taught: Fulfillment is not a goal
to achieve, but always the by-product of a sacrifice.

ELISABETH ELLIOT

If God chooses to remain silent,
your faith should remain content.

RUTH BELL GRAHAM

Those who hunger and thirst for righteousness
are blessed, for they will be filled.

MATTHEW 5:6 HCSB

16

Generosity

He Instructs Us to Be Generous

*So let each one give as he purposes
in his heart, not grudgingly or of necessity;
for God loves a cheerful giver.*

II Corinthians 9:7 NKJV

Dear Lord, You have promised that You love a cheerful giver. And Your Word teaches us that it is more blessed to give than to receive. I pray that my children will give generously and cheerfully of their time, their talents, and their resources. Make them faithful stewards of Your gifts and let them share their gifts with others.

Heavenly Father, Your gifts are priceless. You gave Your Son, Jesus, to save us, and Your motivation was love. I pray that the gifts we give to others will come from an overflow of our hearts, and that they will echo the great love You have for all of Your children.

Amen.

More from God's Word

You should remember the words of the Lord Jesus:
"It is more blessed to give than to receive."

ACTS 20:35 NLT

Remember this: The person who sows sparingly
will also reap sparingly, and the person
who sows generously will also reap generously.

II CORINTHIANS 9:6 HCSB

If you have two shirts, give one to the poor.
If you have food, share it with those who are hungry.

LUKE 3:11 NLT

Therefore, whenever we have the opportunity,
we should do good to everyone—
especially to those in the family of faith.

GALATIANS 6:10 NLT

Truly I tell you, whatever you did for one of the least
of these brothers and sisters of mine, you did for me.

MATTHEW 25:40 NIV

About Generosity

*The goodness you receive from God is a treasure
for you to share with others.*

ELIZABETH GEORGE

*It's what you sow that multiplies,
not what you keep in the barn.*

ADRIAN ROGERS

*When somebody needs a helping hand, he doesn't
need it tomorrow or the next day. He needs it now,
and that's exactly when you should offer to help.
Good deeds, if they are really good,
happen sooner rather than later.*

MARIE T. FREEMAN

*A cheerful giver does not count the cost
of what he gives. His heart is set on pleasing
and cheering him to whom the gift is given.*

JULIAN OF NORWICH

Freely you have received; freely give.

MATTHEW 10:8 NIV

17

God First

Putting God First

But seek first the kingdom of God and His righteousness,
and all these things will be provided for you.

MATTHEW 6:33 HCSB

Dear Lord, I pray that my children will put You first. I pray that they will seek Your kingdom and Your righteousness, and I pray that they will be blessed because of their choices.

Heavenly Father, You know that this world offers countless temptations and distractions. These worldly priorities threaten to sap our energy, monopolize our time, and dominate our thoughts. Protect us from these dangers, Lord, and guide us along the path that You have chosen for us.

You have blessed my family beyond measure, Lord. I pray that we will always put You first, ahead of every other priority.

Amen.

More from God's Word

*Abundant peace belongs to those who love
Your instruction; nothing makes them stumble.*

PSALM 119:165 HCSB

*Be joyful in hope, patient in affliction,
faithful in prayer.*

ROMANS 12:12 NIV

*Those who love Your law have great peace,
and nothing causes them to stumble.*

PSALM 119:165 NASB

Therefore let everyone who is faithful pray to You. . . .

PSALM 32:6 HCSB

*Therefore everyone who hears these words
of mine and puts them into practice is like
a wise man who built his house on the rock.*

MATTHEW 7:24–25 NIV

About Faithfulness

Faith and obedience are bound up
in the same bundle. He that obeys God, trusts God;
and he that trusts God, obeys God.

C. H. SPURGEON

Watch where Jesus went. The one dominant note in his
life was to do his Father's will. His is not the way
of wisdom or of success, but the way of faithfulness.

OSWALD CHAMBERS

You may not always see immediate results,
but all God wants is your obedience and faithfulness.

VONETTE BRIGHT

Faithfulness today is the best preparation
for the demands of tomorrow.

ELISABETH ELLIOT

He who follows righteousness and mercy finds life,
righteousness, and honor.

PROVERBS 21:21 NKJV

18

God's Blessings

Blessings from the Lord

The LORD is gracious and compassionate,
slow to anger and great in faithful love.
The LORD is good to everyone;
His compassion rests on all He has made.

PSALM 145:8–9 HCSB

Dear Lord, I pray that my children will accept Your blessings and receive Your gifts. And I pray that they will follow closely in the footsteps of Your only begotten Son.

You have given my family so much, Father, and we are eternally grateful. We will spend all eternity praising You.

I know, Lord, that You are the Giver of all good gifts. And I know that every good gift You give me is meant to be shared with others. Today, I pray that every member of my family will share Your blessings with others, just as You first shared them with us.

Amen.

More from God's Word

You will show me the path of life;
in Your presence is fullness of joy;
at Your right hand are pleasures forevermore.

Psalm 16:11 NKJV

The Lord is good to all: and his tender mercies
are over all his works.

Psalm 145:9 KJV

The Lord is my rock, my fortress, and my deliverer,
my God, my mountain where I seek refuge.
My shield, the horn of my salvation,
my stronghold, my refuge, and my Savior.

II Samuel 22:2–3 HCSB

The Lord is my shepherd; I shall not want.

Psalm 23:1 KJV

Blessings crown the head of the righteous. . . .

Proverbs 10:6 NIV

About God's Blessings

God is the giver, and we are the receivers.
And His richest gifts are bestowed not upon
those who do the greatest things, but upon those
who accept His abundance and His grace.

HANNAH WHITALL SMITH

How ridiculous to grasp for future gifts when today's
are set before you. Receive today's gift gratefully,
unwrapping it tenderly and delving into its depths.

SARAH YOUNG

God's gifts put man's best dreams to shame.

ELIZABETH BARRETT BROWNING

God is always trying to give good things to us,
but our hands are too full to receive them.

SAINT AUGUSTINE

May Yahweh bless you and protect you; may Yahweh
make His face shine on you and be gracious to you.

NUMBERS 6:24–25 HCSB

19

God's Faithfulness

The Promise of Faithfulness

For Yahweh is good, and His love is eternal;
His faithfulness endures through all generations.

PSALM 100:5 HCSB

Dear Lord, You have promised to be faithful to every generation. Thank You, Father, for Your faithfulness and Your love.

I pray that my children will be faithful to You, Lord. Let them be obedient. Let them live righteously every day of their lives, and let them follow as closely as they can in the footsteps of Your Son.

Today, Lord, I pray that my family will rest in the knowledge of Your constant love. And I pray that they will serve You with willing hands and loving hearts.

Amen.

More from God's Word

Great is thy faithfulness.

LAMENTATIONS 3:23 KJV

God is faithful; you were called by Him
into fellowship with His Son, Jesus Christ our Lord.

I CORINTHIANS 1:9 HCSB

I will sing about the LORD's faithful love forever;
I will proclaim Your faithfulness
to all generations with my mouth.

PSALM 89:1 HCSB

God, You are my God; I eagerly seek You.
I thirst for You . . . My lips will glorify You
because Your faithful love is better than life.

PSALM 63:1, 3 HCSB

For the LORD is good; His mercy is everlasting,
and His truth endures to all generations.

PSALM 100:5 NKJV

About God's Faithfulness

Our prospects are as bright as the promises of God.

ADONIRAM JUDSON

God is faithful even when his children are not.

MAX LUCADO

God is, and all is well.

JOHN GREENLEAF WHITTIER

*Don't let obstacles along the road to eternity
shake your confidence in God's promises.*

DAVID JEREMIAH

*Trials are not enemies of faith but opportunities
to reveal God's faithfulness.*

BARBARA JOHNSON

*Praise the LORD, all nations! Glorify Him,
all peoples! For His faithful love to us is great;
the LORD's faithfulness endures forever. Hallelujah!*

PSALM 117 HCSB

20

God's Guidance

He Promises to Guide Us

The Lord says, "I will guide you along
the best pathway for your life.
I will advise you and watch over you."

<small>Psalm 32:8 NLT</small>

Dear Lord, I pray that my children will seek Your guidance in every aspect of their lives. You have promised to guide them along a path of Your choosing. I pray that they will follow Your lead. And I pray that they will follow closely in the footsteps of Your Son.

I pray that my children will draw near to You, Father, with the confidence that You will lead them to a place of abundance and peace. And as they make that journey, let them share Your good news with all who cross my path.

Amen.

More from God's Word

Yet LORD, You are our Father;
we are the clay, and You are our potter;
we all are the work of Your hands.

ISAIAH 64:8 HCSB

Teach me to do Your will, for You are my God;
Your Spirit is good. Lead me in the land of uprightness.

PSALM 143:10 NKJV

Shew me thy ways, O LORD; teach me thy paths.
Lead me in thy truth, and teach me: for thou art
the God of my salvation; on thee do I wait all the day.

PSALM 25:4–5 KJV

Morning by morning he wakens me and opens
my understanding to his will. The Sovereign LORD
has spoken to me, and I have listened.

ISAIAH 50:4–5 NLT

Direct your children onto the right path,
and when they are older, they will not leave it.

PROVERBS 22:6 NLT

About God's Guidance

*God never leads us to do anything
that is contrary to the Bible.*

BILLY GRAHAM

*I am satisfied that when the Almighty
wants me to do or not to do any particular thing,
he finds a way to let me know it.*

ABRAHAM LINCOLN

*As you walk through the valley of the unknown,
you will find the footprints of Jesus
both in front of you and beside you.*

CHARLES STANLEY

*We have ample evidence that the Lord is able to guide.
The promises cover every imaginable situation.
All we need to do is to take the hand he stretches out.*

ELISABETH ELLIOT

*Trust in the LORD with all your heart,
And lean not on your own understanding;
In all your ways acknowledge Him,
And He shall direct your paths.*

PROVERBS 3:5–6 NKJV

21

God's Help

He Promises to Care

*The L*ORD *is good to those who wait for Him,*
to the person who seeks Him.

LAMENTATIONS 3:25 HCSB

I thank You, Lord, for Your love, for Your protection, and for Your care. Your love endures forever, and I pray that my children will accept Your blessings with open arms and grateful hearts.

Dear Lord, You have given my children special talents and unique opportunities for service. I ask that You lead them along the path You have chosen. Give them the wisdom to know Your plan and the courage to follow wherever You may lead.

You care for my family, Father, and I am grateful. I will praise You today, tomorrow, and forever.

Amen.

More from God's Word

*The L*ORD *is my strength and my song;*
He has become my salvation.

EXODUS 15:2 HCSB

For I, Yahweh your God, hold your right hand
and say to you: Do not fear, I will help you.

ISAIAH 41:13 HCSB

*Wait on the L*ORD*, and He will rescue you.*

PROVERBS 20:22 HCSB

So we can be sure when we say,
"I will not be afraid, because the Lord is my helper.
People can't do anything to me."

HEBREWS 13:6 NCV

Ask, and it will be given to you; seek,
and you will find; knock, and it will be opened to you.
For everyone who asks receives, and he who seeks
finds, and to him who knocks it will be opened.

MATTHEW 7:7–8 NKJV

About God's Help and Care

Faith is not merely holding on to God.
It is God holding on to you.

CORRIE TEN BOOM

The safest place in all the world
is in the will of God, and the safest protection
in all the world is the name of God.

WARREN WIERSBE

God will give us the strength and resources we need
to live through any situation in life that He ordains.

BILLY GRAHAM

Once we recognize our need for Jesus, then the building
of our faith begins. It is a daily, moment-by-moment
life of absolute dependence upon Him for everything.

CATHERINE MARSHALL

Peace, peace to you, and peace to him who helps you,
for your God helps you.

I CHRONICLES 12:18 HCSB

22

God's Love

The Promise of God's Love

Give thanks to Him and praise His name.
For Yahweh is good, and His love is eternal;
His faithfulness endures through all generations.

PSALM 100:4–5 HCSB

Dear God, I thank You for Your love. Your love endures forever and Your faithfulness extends throughout all generations. I pray that my children will love You, Father, and I ask that they demonstrate their love through obedience to Your commandments.

I pray that my children will continue to grow in their love for You, Father, and I pray that they will share Your love and Your message with a world that needs both.

Amen.

More from God's Word

We love him, because he first loved us.

I John 4:19 KJV

For He is gracious and compassionate,
slow to anger, rich in faithful love.

Joel 2:13 HCSB

For God so loved the world, that he gave his only
begotten Son, that whosoever believeth in him
should not perish, but have everlasting life.

John 3:16 KJV

The Lord's lovingkindnesses indeed never cease,
for His compassions never fail. They are new
every morning; great is Your faithfulness.

Lamentations 3:22–23 NASB

About God's Love

The greatest sense of love, which is available
for us at all times, is God's love.

STORMIE OMARTIAN

There is no pit so deep that God's love
is not deeper still.

CORRIE TEN BOOM

God proved His love on the cross.
When Christ hung, and bled, and died,
it was God saying to the world, "I love you."

BILLY GRAHAM

We do not need to beg Him to bless us;
He simply cannot help it.

HANNAH WHITALL SMITH

And we have known and believed the love
that God has for us. God is love, and he who abides
in love abides in God, and God in him.

I JOHN 4:16 NKJV

23

God's Power

God's Awesome Power

For the LORD your God is the God
of gods and LORD of lords,
the great, mighty, and awesome God.

DEUTERONOMY 10:17 HCSB

Dear Lord, I pray that my children will respect Your awesome power. Nothing, absolutely nothing, is impossible for You. I pray that they will develop a healthy respect for Your power, Your truth, Your love, and Your Son.

Because Your power is limitless, Father, I know that You perform miracles when it serves Your purpose. I pray that my children will open their eyes—and their hearts—to the miracles You perform. The heavens declare Your glory, Father. I pray that my children will declare Your glory too.

Amen.

More from God's Word

Is anything impossible for the LORD?

GENESIS 18:14 HCSB

But Jesus looked at them and said, "With men this is impossible, but with God all things are possible."

MATTHEW 19:26 HCSB

Depend on the LORD and his strength; always go to him for help. Remember the miracles he has done; remember his wonders and his decisions.

PSALM 105:4–5 NCV

You are the God of miracles and wonders! You demonstrate your awesome power among the nations.

PSALM 77:14 NLT

For the Kingdom of God is not just a lot of talk; it is living by God's power.

I CORINTHIANS 4:20 NLT

About God's Power

If you are strangers to prayer,
you are strangers to power.

BILLY SUNDAY

The power of God through His Spirit will work
within us to the degree that we permit it.

LETTIE COWMAN

Of course you will encounter trouble.
But behold a God of power who can
take any evil and turn it into a door of hope.

CATHERINE MARSHALL

Like dynamite, God's power is only latent power
until it is released. You can release God's
dynamite power into people's lives and the world
through faith, your words, and prayer.

BILL BRIGHT

His divine power has given us everything we need
for life and godliness through our knowledge of him
who called us by his own glory and goodness.

II PETER 1:3 NIV

24

God's Presence

He Promises Never to Leave Us

I know the LORD is always with me.
I will not be shaken, for he is right beside me.

PSALM 16:8 NLT

Dear Lord, I pray that my children will sense Your presence. You have promised to be with them always. Because my children are never alone, they can face the challenges of this world with hope and assurance.

Heavenly Father, You are already everywhere my family has ever been and every place we will ever be. Please let us draw strength from You. Help us feel Your presence in every situation and in every circumstance. You are nearer to us than the air that we breathe. We praise You and thank You, Lord, today and forever.

Amen.

More from God's Word

Be still, and know that I am God. . . .

PSALM 46:10 KJV

Draw near to God, and He will draw near to you.

JAMES 4:8 HCSB

Though I walk through the valley of the shadow of death, I will fear no evil: for thou art with me.

PSALM 23:4 KJV

For He looks to the ends of the earth and sees everything under the heavens.

JOB 28:24 HCSB

I am not alone, because the Father is with Me.

JOHN 16:32 NKJV

About God's Presence

God is an infinite circle whose center is everywhere.

SAINT. AUGUSTINE

*To experience joy on a daily basis, learn what it means
to live in the moment. Living in the moment helps
us recognize that God can be found in this moment,
whether it contains joy or sorrow.*

KAY WARREN

*You need not cry very loudly;
he is nearer to us than we think.*

BROTHER LAWRENCE

*Do not limit the limitless God! With Him,
face the future unafraid because you are never alone.*

LETTIE COWMAN

*For the eyes of Yahweh roam throughout the earth
to show Himself strong for those whose hearts are
completely His. You have been foolish in this matter.
Therefore, you will have wars from now on.*

II CHRONICLES 16:9 HCSB

25

God's Promises

He Keeps His Promises

*Sustain me as You promised, and I will live;
do not let me be ashamed of my hope.*

Psalm 119:116 HCSB

I thank you, Lord, for Your promises; they are the anchor of my hope. I pray that my children will trust Your promises and demonstrate their trust through obedience, through gratitude, and through praise for You.

I pray that my children will use the Bible as their guidebook for life, and I pray that they will trust You, Father, to speak to them through Your Holy Spirit and through Your holy Word.

You have so much to teach us, Lord. May we continue to grow spiritually, and may we continue to follow Your Son today, tomorrow, and forever.

Amen.

More from God's Word

As for God, his way is perfect:
the word of the LORD is tried: he is a buckler
to all those that trust in him.

PSALM 18:30 KJV

They will bind themselves to the LORD
with an eternal covenant that will never be forgotten.

JEREMIAH 50:5 NLT

My God is my rock, in whom I take refuge,
my shield and the horn of my salvation.

II SAMUEL 22:3 NIV

He heeded their prayer,
because they put their trust in him.

I CHRONICLES 5:20 NKJV

The LORD is good to those whose hope is in him,
to the one who seeks him.

LAMENTATIONS 3:25 NIV

About God's Promises

Gather the riches of God's promises.
Nobody can take away from you those texts
from the Bible which you have learned by heart.

CORRIE TEN BOOM

Faith is the assurance that the thing which God
has said in His word is true, and that God
will act according to what He has said.

GEORGE MÜELLER

The Bible is God's book of promises, and unlike
the books of man, it does not change or go out of date.

BILLY GRAHAM

Beloved, God's promises can never fail to be accomplished,
and those who patiently wait can never be disappointed,
for a believing faith leads to realization.

LETTIE COWMAN

Let us hold on to the confession of our hope
without wavering, for He who promised is faithful.

HEBREWS 10:23 HCSB

26

God's Protection

He Has Promised to Protect Us

*The LORD is my light and my salvation—
whom should I fear? The LORD is the stronghold
of my life—of whom should I be afraid?*

PSALM 27:1 HCSB

Dear Lord, You are my salvation. You have promised to protect me and my family, so we have nothing to fear.

I thank You for Your protection, and I pray that my children will entrust their lives to You. When they do, they are secure.

Sometimes life is difficult. But when we lift our eyes to You, Father, You strengthen us. When we are weak, You lift us up. When we are fearful, You give us hope. Today and every day, let us turn to You for strength, for hope, and for direction.

Amen.

More from God's Word

As for God, His way is perfect; the word of the LORD is proven; He is a shield to all who trust in Him.

PSALM 18:30 NKJV

The LORD is my rock, my fortress, and my deliverer, my God, my mountain where I seek refuge. My shield, the horn of my salvation, my stronghold, my refuge, and my Savior.

II SAMUEL 22:2–3 HCSB

Those who trust in the LORD are like Mount Zion. It cannot be shaken; it remains forever.

PSALM 125:1 HCSB

So we may boldly say: "The LORD is my helper; I will not fear. What can man do to me?"

HEBREWS 13:6 NKJV

But the LORD has been my defense, and my God the rock of my refuge.

PSALM 94:22 NKJV

About God's Protection

A mighty fortress is our God, a bulwark never failing,
our helper he amid the flood of mortal ills prevailing.

MARTIN LUTHER

God is trying to get a message through to you,
and the message is: "Stop depending on inadequate
human resources. Let me handle the matter."

CATHERINE MARSHALL

Only believe, don't fear. Our Master, Jesus,
always watches over us, and no matter what
the persecution, Jesus will surely overcome it.

LOTTIE MOON

The safest place in all the world
is in the will of God, and the safest protection
in all the world is the name of God.

WARREN WIERSBE

The LORD is my shepherd, I shall not want.
He makes me lie down in green pastures;
He leads me beside quiet waters. He restores my soul.

PSALM 23:1–3 NASB

27

God's Provision

He Has Promised
to Provide for Our Needs

Our help is in the name of the LORD,
Who made heaven and earth.

PSALM 124:8 NASB

Dear Lord, You have promised to provide for Your children. I thank You, Father, and I pray that my children will seek Your protection and Your support in good times and in hard times.

I thank You, Father, for the love You have shown my family and for the blessings You have given us. You are our Shepherd, Lord, and we are the sheep of Your pasture.

Help us to lean not upon our own understanding, but upon You. Keep us mindful, Lord, of Your protection, Your provision, and Your love, now and forever.

Amen.

More from God's Word

Don't be afraid, because I am your God.
I will make you strong and will help you;
I will support you with my right hand that saves you.

ISAIAH 41:10 NCV

I will give you a new heart
and put a new spirit within you.

EZEKIEL 36:26 HCSB

I was helpless, and He saved me.

PSALM 116:6 HCSB

Put on the full armor of God so that you
can stand against the tactics of the Devil.

EPHESIANS 6:11 HCSB

God is my shield, saving those
whose hearts are true and right.

PSALM 7:10 NLT

About God's Provision

Put your hand into the hand of God. He gives
the calmness and serenity of heart and soul.

LETTIE COWMAN

God is, must be, our answer to every question
and every cry of need.

HANNAH WHITALL SMITH

Our Lord never drew power from Himself;
He drew it always from His Father.

OSWALD CHAMBERS

Claim all of God's promises in the Bible.
Your sins, your worries, your life—
you may cast them all on Him.

CORRIE TEN BOOM

Be strong and courageous, and do the work.
Don't be afraid or discouraged by the size of the task,
for the LORD God, my God, is with you.
He will not fail you or forsake you.

I CHRONICLES 28:20 NLT

28

God's Sufficiency

He Is Sufficient
to Meet Our Needs

*My grace is sufficient for you,
for my power is made perfect in weakness.*

II CORINTHIANS 12:9 NIV

Dear Lord, I pray that my children will never forget that You are sufficient to meet their needs. I pray that they will seek Your guidance and Your protection in every circumstance and in every season of life.

I pray that they will turn to You, Lord, when they are anxious or fearful. You are their loving heavenly Father, sufficient in all things; may they trust You always.

Today, I will entrust to You the challenges that are simply too big for me to solve. And I earnestly pray, dear Lord, that my children will do the same.

Amen.

More from God's Word

And my God will supply all your needs
according to His riches in glory in Christ Jesus.

PHILIPPIANS 4:19 HCSB

For the eyes of the LORD are on the righteous,
And His ears are open to their prayers;
But the face of the LORD is against those who do evil.

I PETER 3:12 NKJV

And God is able to make every grace overflow to you,
so that in every way, always having everything you
need, you may excel in every good work.

II CORINTHIANS 9:8 HCSB

The Lord is my strength and song,
And He has become my salvation;
He is my God, and I will praise Him.

EXODUS 15:2 NKJV

Take up My yoke and learn from Me, because I am
gentle and humble in heart, and you will find rest for
yourselves. For My yoke is easy and My burden is light.

MATTHEW 11:29–30 HCSB

About God's Sufficiency
and Earthly Success

Never imagine that you can be
a loser by trusting in God.

C. H. SPURGEON

Aim at heaven and you get earth thrown in.
Aim at earth and you get neither.

C. S. LEWIS

Success or failure can be pretty well predicted
by the degree to which the heart is fully in it.

JOHN ELDREDGE

The measure of a life, after all,
is not its duration but its donation.

CORRIE TEN BOOM

For I know the thoughts that I think toward you,
says the LORD, thoughts of peace and not of evil, to give
you a future and a hope. Then you will call upon Me
and go and pray to Me, and I will listen to you.

JEREMIAH 29:11–12 NKJV

29

God's Support

He Has Promised to Support His Children

And my God will supply all your needs according to His riches in glory in Christ Jesus.

PHILIPPIANS 4:19 HCSB

Dear Lord, I pray that my children will always lean on You for strength. And I pray that they will depend upon You to meet their needs. You will never leave nor forsake them. You are always with them, Father, protecting them, encouraging them, and supporting them.

You have promised to supply my family with the things we really need. Through good times and hard times, You have provided for us, Lord, and we will praise You for Your love, for Your strength, and for Your protection.

Amen.

More from God's Word

For the eyes of the LORD are on the righteous,
And His ears are open to their prayers;
But the face of the LORD is against those who do evil.

I PETER 3:12 NKJV

And God is able to make every grace overflow
to you, so that in every way, always having everything
you need, you may excel in every good work.

II CORINTHIANS 9:8 HCSB

The Lord is my strength and song,
And He has become my salvation;
He is my God, and I will praise Him.

EXODUS 15:2 NKJV

Take up My yoke and learn from Me,
because I am gentle and humble in heart,
and you will find rest for yourselves.
For My yoke is easy and My burden is light.

MATTHEW 11:29–30 HCSB

About God's Sufficiency

God is sufficient for all our needs, for every problem,
for every difficulty, for every broken heart,
and for every human sorrow.

PETER MARSHALL

The strength that we claim from God's Word
does not depend on circumstances. Circumstances
will be difficult, but our strength will be sufficient.

CORRIE TEN BOOM

God's saints in all ages have realized that God
was enough for them. God is enough for time;
God is enough for eternity. God is enough!

HANNAH WHITALL SMITH

We have no sufficient strength of our own.
All our sufficiency is of God.

MATTHEW HENRY

My grace is sufficient for you, for my power
is made perfect in weakness.

II CORINTHIANS 12:9 NIV

30

Holiness

He Calls Us to Be Holy

*But seek first the kingdom of God
and His righteousness,
and all these things shall be added to you.*

MATTHEW 6:33 NKJV

Dear Lord, You are holy, and You have promised that if we seek Your kingdom and Your righteousness, we will be blessed.

I pray that my children will live righteously as they follow in the footsteps of Your Son. And I pray that You will bless them and keep them, now and forever.

I pray that each member of my family honors You and praises You, Father. Make us Your faithful servants, and let us share the joyous news of Jesus Christ with a world that needs His healing touch this day and every day.

Amen.

More from God's Word

The pure in heart are blessed,
for they will see God.

MATTHEW 5:8 HCSB

Flee from youthful passions,
and pursue righteousness, faith, love,
and peace, along with those who call
on the Lord from a pure heart.

II TIMOTHY 2:22 HCSB

The highway of the upright avoids evil;
the one who guards his way protects his life.

PROVERBS 16:17 HCSB

He who follows righteousness and mercy
finds life, righteousness, and honor.

PROVERBS 21:21 NKJV

For the LORD knows the way of the righteous,
but the way of the ungodly shall perish.

PSALM 1:6 NKJV

About Holiness

Holiness, not happiness, is the chief end of man.

<small>OSWALD CHAMBERS</small>

Heroism is an extraordinary feat of the flesh;
holiness is an ordinary act of the spirit. One may bring
personal glory; the other always gives God glory.

<small>CHARLES COLSON</small>

Mark it down—your progress in holiness will never
exceed your relationship with the holy Word of God.

<small>NANCY LEIGH DEMOSS</small>

Living the Christian life means striving for holiness.

<small>BILLY GRAHAM</small>

Sin will grow without cultivation,
but holiness needs cultivation.

<small>C. H. SPURGEON</small>

Live peaceful and quiet lives
in all godliness and holiness.

<small>I TIMOTHY 2:2 NIV</small>

31

Holy Spirit

The Promise of the Holy Spirit

And I will pray the Father, and He will give you another
Helper, that He may abide with you forever—
the Spirit of truth, whom the world cannot receive,
because it neither sees Him nor knows Him; but you
know Him, for He dwells with you and will be in you.
I will not leave you orphans; I will come to you.

JOHN 14:16–18 NKJV

Dear Lord, I thank You for sending the Holy Spirit, the Spirit of truth, who stands ready to help us interpret Your Word and understand Your intentions. I pray that my children will welcome the Holy Spirit into their hearts and that they will live by the Spirit in every season of life.

Heavenly Father, I want to grow closer to You each day, and I seek the same for my children. Let us trust the Holy Spirit to lead us along a path of Your choosing, Father, as we strive to obey Your commandments and follow in the footsteps of Your Son.

Amen.

More from God's Word

There are diversities of gifts, but the same Spirit.

I CORINTHIANS 12:4 NKJV

Human life comes from human parents,
but spiritual life comes from the Spirit.

JOHN 3:6 NCV

Since we live by the Spirit,
we must also follow the Spirit.

GALATIANS 5:25 HCSB

Now the Lord is the Spirit,
and where the Spirit of the Lord is,
there is freedom.

II CORINTHIANS 3:17 HCSB

Now God has revealed these things
to us by the Spirit, for the Spirit searches everything,
even the deep things of God.

I CORINTHIANS 2:10 HCSB

About the Holy Spirit

*The maturity of a Christian experience
cannot be reached in a moment, but is the result
of the work of God's Holy Spirit, who, by His
energizing and transforming power, causes us
to grow up into Christ in all things.*

HANNAH WHITALL SMITH

*God calls us to do his work, proclaiming his Word to
people he loves under the anointing power of the Holy
Spirit to produce results that only he can bring about.*

JIM CYMBALA

*The power of God through His Spirit will work
within us to the degree that we permit it.*

LETTIE COWMAN

*Now may the God of hope fill you with all joy
and peace as you believe in Him so that you may overflow with hope by the power of the Holy Spirit.*

ROMANS 15:13 HCSB

32

Humility

He Promises to Reward Humility

Therefore humble yourselves under the mighty hand of God, that He may exalt you in due time, casting all your care upon Him, for He cares for you.

I Peter 5:6–7 NKJV

Dear Lord, I pray that my children will be humble, modest, and unpretentious. Your Word teaches us to be humble, but the world tempts us to be prideful. Help us to guard our hearts against the sin of pride.

Keep us humble, Father. Let us grow beyond my need for earthly praise, and let us look only to You for approval.

Jesus clothed Himself with humility. Today and every day, let my children and me follow His example. Christ came to this earth so that He might live and die for us. Clothe us in humility, Lord, so that I might be more like Your Son.

Amen.

More from God's Word

Always be humble, gentle, and patient,
accepting each other in love.

Ephesians 4:2 NCV

Humble yourselves in the sight of the Lord,
and he shall lift you up.

James 4:10 KJV

For everyone who exalts himself
will be humbled,
and the one who humbles himself
will be exalted.

Luke 14:11 HCSB

Therefore, God's chosen ones, holy and loved,
put on heartfelt compassion, kindness,
humility, gentleness, and patience.

Colossians 3:12 HCSB

Blessed are the meek: for they shall inherit the earth.

Matthew 5:5 KJV

About Humility

Pride builds walls between people,
humility builds bridges.

RICK WARREN

Nothing sets a person so much
out of the Devil's reach as humility.

JONATHAN EDWARDS

Not until we have become humble and teachable, standing
in awe of God's holiness and sovereignty, distrusting
our own thoughts, and willing to have our minds turned
upside down, can divine wisdom become ours.

J. I. PACKER

God measures people by the small dimensions
of humility and not by the bigness of their
achievements or the size of their capabilities.

BILLY GRAHAM

You rescue the humble, but your eyes watch
the proud and humiliate them.

II SAMUEL 22:28 NLT

33

Integrity

Honest Relationships

The one who lives with integrity lives securely,
but whoever perverts his ways will be found out.

<small>PROVERBS 10:9 HCSB</small>

Dear Lord, I pray that my children will have honest, meaningful relationships. I pray that they will understand the value of integrity and the importance of trust.

Heavenly Father, You have promised us that when we live with integrity, You will protect us. Your Word teaches us that with honesty comes security. And You warn us that dishonesty will be found out and punished.

I pray that my children will understand these lessons, Lord, and I pray that they will honor You by speaking truthfully and behaving honorably this day and every day.

Amen.

More from God's Word

Good people will be guided by honesty;
dishonesty will destroy those
who are not trustworthy.

PROVERBS 11:3 NCV

The good people who live honest lives
will be a blessing to their children.

PROVERBS 20:7 NCV

A righteous man is careful in dealing
with his neighbor, but the ways
of the wicked lead them astray.

PROVERBS 12:26 HCSB

Dishonest scales are detestable to the LORD,
but an accurate weight is His delight.

PROVERBS 11:1 HCSB

Let your "Yes" be "Yes," and your "No," "No."

MATTHEW 5:37 NKJV

About Truth and Integrity

The single most important element
in any human relationship is honesty—
with oneself, with God, and with others.

CATHERINE MARSHALL

Indeed, it is not in human nature to deceive others
for any long period of time without in a measure
deceiving ourselves too.

JOHN HENRY CARDINAL NEWMAN

The commandment of absolute truthfulness
is only another name for the fullness of discipleship.

DIETRICH BONHOEFFER

God is much more concerned about your character
than your career, because you will take
your character into eternity, but not your career.

RICK WARREN

And ye shall know the truth,
and the truth shall make you free.

JOHN 8:32 KJV

34

Jesus

Following in Christ's Footsteps

*Whoever wants to be my disciple must deny themselves
and take up their cross and follow me.*

MARK 8:34 NIV

Heavenly Father, Your Word promises that Jesus died so that we who follow Him can live eternally with Him. I am humbled by Christ's love and by His sacrifice. And I pray that my children will follow Him, trust Him, and give their lives to Him.

We thank You, Lord, for Your Son and for the priceless gift of eternal life. You loved us first, and we will return Your love today, tomorrow, and forever.

I praise You, Father, for a love that never ends. And I pray that my children will know Your Son and share His love with the world.

Amen.

More from God's Word

But whoever keeps His word, truly the love of God
is perfected in him. By this we know that we
are in Him. He who says he abides in Him
ought himself also to walk just as He walked.

I JOHN 2:5–6 NKJV

Therefore as you have received Christ Jesus the Lord,
walk in Him, rooted and built up in Him
and established in the faith, just as you were taught,
overflowing with gratitude.

COLOSSIANS 2:6–7 HCSB

I tell you the truth, whoever believes in me
will do the same things that I do.
Those who believe will do even greater things than
these, because I am going to the Father.

JOHN 14:12 NCV

Therefore, if anyone is in Christ,
he is a new creature; the old things
have passed away, and look, new things have come.

II CORINTHIANS 5:17 HCSB

About Knowing Jesus

*Consider Jesus. Know Jesus. Learn what kind
of Person it is you say you trust and love
and worship. Soak in the shadow of Jesus.
Saturate your soul with the ways of Jesus.
Watch Him. Listen to Him. Stand in awe of Him.*

JOHN PIPER

*Jesus is Victor. Calvary is the place of victory.
Obedience is the pathway of victory. Bible study
and prayer are the preparation for victory.*

CORRIE TEN BOOM

*Not only do we not know God except through
Jesus Christ; we do not even know ourselves
except through Jesus Christ.*

BLAISE PASCAL

*But we do see Jesus—made lower than the angels
for a short time so that by God's grace he might
taste death for everyone—crowned with glory and hon-
or because of His suffering in death.*

HEBREWS 2:9 HCSB

35

Knowing God

Knowing Him

*The one who does not love
does not know God, for God is love.*

I JOHN 4:8 NASB

Heavenly Father, Your Word teaches us that You are love. I pray that my children will know You and experience Your love. And because I love my children, I pray that they will be true disciples of Your Son.

Dear Lord, I ask that You give my children the wisdom to seek You, the patience to wait for You, the insight to hear Your voice, and the courage to obey You. When they trust You completely, Father, and when they give themselves to You, they are secure. I pray that they will sense Your presence, study Your Word, obey Your commandments, and follow Your Son this day and every day.

Amen.

More from God's Word

Supplement your faith with a generous provision of moral excellence, and moral excellence with knowledge, and knowledge with self-control, and self-control with patient endurance, and patient endurance with godliness. .

II P<small>ETER</small> 1:5–6 NLT

Seek the L<small>ORD</small> while He may be found; call to Him while He is near.

I<small>SAIAH</small> 55:6 HCSB

Seek the L<small>ORD</small> and live. . . .

A<small>MOS</small> 5:6 NKJV

Be silent before Me.

I<small>SAIAH</small> 41:1 HCSB

Speak, L<small>ORD</small>. I am your servant and I am listening.

I S<small>AMUEL</small> 3:10 NCV

About Knowing God

*Getting to know God and being able to call on Him
is the most important step in storing up for the storms.*

BILLY GRAHAM

*God speaks through a variety of means. In the present,
God primarily speaks by the Holy Spirit, through
the Bible, prayer, circumstances, and the church.*

HENRY BLACKABY

*What were we made for? To know God.
What aim should we have in life? To know God.
What is the eternal life that Jesus gives? To know God.
What is the best thing in life? To know God.*

J. I. PACKER

*As we come to know God better, we will also find it
easier to know, follow, and accept His will for our life.*

ELIZABETH GEORGE

*Honor His holy name; let the hearts of those
who seek Yahweh rejoice. Search for the LORD
and for His strength; seek His face always.*

I CHRONICLES 16:10–11 HCSB

36

Learning

Listen and Learn

I will instruct you and show you the way to go;
with My eye on you, I will give counsel.

Psalm 32:8 HCSB

Dear Lord, I pray that my children will hear Your voice and trust Your wisdom. And I pray that they continue to learn through every stage of life. We all have so much to learn, Lord, and we have so little time. So I pray that my children will be quick to learn the lessons You intend to teach them.

I pray that my children will read Your Word, hear Your voice, and follow Your path through every stage of life.

Let us seek Your wisdom, Father, and live by it. When we trust in the wisdom of the world, we are often led astray, but when we trust You, we build our lives upon a firm foundation. Thank You, Lord, for Your wisdom.

Amen.

More from God's Word

Commit yourself to instruction; listen carefully
to words of knowledge.

PROVERBS 23:12 NLT

Enthusiasm without knowledge is not good.
If you act too quickly, you might make a mistake.

PROVERBS 19:2 NCV

Joyful is the person who finds wisdom,
the one who gains understanding.

PROVERBS 3:13 NLT

Teach me Your way, Yahweh,
and I will live by Your truth.
Give me an undivided mind to fear Your name.

PSALM 86:11 HCSB

Anyone who listens to my teaching
and follows it is wise, like a person
who builds a house on solid rock.

MATTHEW 7:24 NLT

About Learning

True learning can take place at every age of life,
and it doesn't have to be in the curriculum plan.

SUZANNE DALE EZELL

Today is yesterday's pupil.

THOMAS FULLER

Each problem is a God-appointed instructor.

CHARLES SWINDOLL

Life is not a holiday but an education. And the one
eternal lesson for all of us is how we can love.

HENRY DRUMMOND

Learning makes a man fit company for himself.

THOMAS FULLER

Wisdom is the principal thing;
Therefore get wisdom.
And in all your getting, get understanding.

PROVERBS 4:7 NKJV

37

Light

The Light of the World

I am the light of the world. Anyone who follows me will never walk in darkness but will have the light of life.

JOHN 8:12 NIV

Dear Lord, Your Word promises that Jesus is the Light of the world. I pray that my children will make Him the Light of their world and the Anchor of their faith.

Jesus asks us to take up His cross and follow Him. When we do, our lives are forever changed. So we must be true disciples, always ready to share His good news and tell of His miraculous love.

Today, Father, I pray that my children will know the truth and that the truth will set them free. And I pray that they will walk in the light of Your Son, now and forever.

Amen.

More from God's Word

I tell you the truth, whoever believes in me
will do the same things that I do. Those who
believe will do even greater things than these,
because I am going to the Father.

John 14:12 NCV

Whoever wants to be my disciple must deny themselves
and take up their cross and follow me.

Mark 8:34 NIV

Therefore, as you have received Christ Jesus the Lord,
walk in Him, rooted and built up in Him
and established in the faith, just as you were taught,
overflowing with gratitude.

Colossians 2:6–7 HCSB

Therefore, if anyone is in Christ,
he is a new creation;
old things have passed away,
and look, new things have come.

II Corinthians 5:17 HCSB

About the Light

God's Word is a light not only to our path
but also to our thinking. Place it in your heart today,
and you will never walk in darkness.

JONI EARECKSON TADA

If we guard some corner of darkness
in ourselves, we will soon be drawing
someone else into darkness, shutting them out
from the light in the face of Jesus Christ.

ELISABETH ELLIOT

Sometimes what seems like the darkest step
we've ever been on comes just before
the brightest light we've ever experienced.

STORMIE OMARTIAN

But we do see Jesus, who was made lower than
the angels for a little while, now crowned with glory
and honor because he suffered death, so that by
the grace of God he might taste death for everyone.

HEBREWS 2:9 NIV

38

Listening to God

Hearing His Voice

Speak, LORD. I am your servant and I am listening.

I SAMUEL 3:10 NCV

Dear Lord, I pray that my children will hear Your voice and trust Your promises. They have so much to learn and You have so much to teach. Give them the wisdom to be still and the discernment to hear Your quiet voice today and every day.

My children live in a noisy world, Lord, filled with distractions, interruptions, and temptations. Their world is brimming with opportunities to stray from Your path. Protect them, Lord.

I pray that You will give my children the wisdom to listen carefully to the only guidance that really matters: Your guidance.

Amen.

More from God's Word

In quietness and in confidence shall be your strength.

ISAIAH 30:15 KJV

Rest in the LORD, and wait patiently for Him.

PSALM 37:7 NKJV

Listen, listen to me,
and eat what is good,
and your soul will delight
in the richest of fare.
Give ear and come to me;
listen, that your soul may live.

ISAIAH 55:2–3 NIV

The one who is from God listens to God's words.
This is why you don't listen,
because you are not from God.

JOHN 8:47 HCSB

Be silent before Me.

ISAIAH 41:1 HCSB

115

About Listening to God

*Prayer is speaking to God, but sometimes He uses our
times of prayerful silence to speak to us in return.*

BILLY GRAHAM

*Some of us can only hear God in the thunder of revivals
or in public worship; we have to learn to listen
to God's voice in the ordinary circumstances of life.*

OSWALD CHAMBERS

*Deep within the center of the soul is a chamber
of peace where God lives, and where,
if we will enter it and quiet all the other sounds,
we can hear His gentle whisper.*

LETTIE COWMAN

*Prayer begins by talking to God,
but it ends in listening to him. In the face
of Absolute Truth, silence is the soul's language.*

FULTON J. SHEEN

Be still, and know that I am God, . . .

PSALM 46:10 KJV

39

Love

And the Greatest of These . . .

And now abide faith, hope, love, these three;
but the greatest of these is love.

I Corinthians 13:13 NKJV

Dear Lord, You have commanded us to love one another. I pray that my children will obey Your commandment today, tomorrow, and every day of their lives.

Your Word teaches us that love is a precious gift. I pray that my children will be able to give that gift and receive it in every stage of life.

Heavenly Father, I pray that my children will acknowledge Your love; I pray that they will accept Your love; and I pray that they will share Your love. And I ask that the love they feel in their hearts be expressed through kind words, good deeds, and sincere prayers.

Amen.

More from God's Word

A new commandment I give unto you,
That ye love one another; as I have loved you,
that ye also love one another.

John 13:34 KJV

Love is patient, love is kind. Love does not envy,
is not boastful, is not conceited.

I Corinthians 13:4 HCSB

Beloved, if God so loved us,
we ought also to love one another.

I John 4:11 KJV

Beyond all these things put on love,
which is the perfect bond of unity.

Colossians 3:14 NASB

You have heard it said, "Love your neighbor
and hate your enemy." But I tell you: Love your
enemies and pray for those who persecute you, that
you may be children of your Father in heaven.

Matthew 5:43–45 NIV

About Love

*The vast ocean of Love cannot be measured
or explained, but it can be experienced.*

SARAH YOUNG

Love always means sacrifice.

ELISABETH ELLIOT

*Show me your hands. Do they have scars from giving?
Show me your feet. Are they wounded in service? Show
me your heart. Have you left a place for divine love?*

FULTON J. SHEEN

*The love life of the Christian is a crucial
battleground. There, if nowhere else,
it will be determined who is Lord: the world,
the self, and the Devil—or the Lord Christ.*

ELISABETH ELLIOT

*Line by line, moment by moment, special times
are etched into our memories in the permanent
ink of everlasting love in our relationships.*

GLORIA GAITHER

40

Miracles

He Promises Miracles

*You are the God of great wonders! You demonstrate
your awesome power among the nations.*

PSALM 77:14 NLT

Dear Lord, nothing is impossible for You. You created
the universe, and You created me. I pray that my children
will recognize Your power and respect it.

If my children ever lose hope, I pray that You will
give them strength. When others lose hope, I pray
that my children will tell them of Your glory and Your
works. Because nothing is impossible for You, Father, I
will pray for miracles and I will work for them. I pray
my children will do the same.

Amen.

More from God's Word

And God confirmed the message by giving signs
and wonders and various miracles and gifts
of the Holy Spirit whenever he chose.

HEBREWS 2:4 NLT

What no eye has seen, what no ear has heard,
and what no human mind has conceived—
the things God has prepared for those who love him.

I CORINTHIANS 2:9 NIV

And Jesus looking upon them saith,
With men it is impossible, but not with God:
for with God all things are possible.

MARK 10:27 KJV

For with God nothing shall be impossible.

LUKE 1:37 KJV

About God's Miraculous Power

God specializes in things thought impossible.

CATHERINE MARSHALL

It is wonderful what miracles God works
in wills that are utterly surrendered to Him.

HANNAH WHITALL SMITH

We honor God by asking for great things
when they are a part of His promise. We dishonor
Him and cheat ourselves when we ask for molehills
where He has promised mountains.

VANCE HAVNER

Are you looking for a miracle?
If you keep your eyes wide open and trust in God,
you won't have to look very far.

MARIE T. FREEMAN

Is anything too hard for the LORD?

GENESIS 18:14 NKJV

41

New Beginnings

The Promise of a Fresh Start

Then the One seated on the throne said,
"Look! I am making everything new."

REVELATION 21:5 HCSB

Dear Lord, nothing is impossible for You. You can wipe away our sins and make us whole again. You can clear away the old and bring forth the new. When we come to You and ask, You renew our spirits and transform our lives.

Heavenly Father, I pray that whenever my children need a fresh start, they will come to You and ask. When they ask, You will answer, and You will make everything new for them.

Lord, I thank You for protecting my family. Let us be worthy stewards of the gifts You've given us. And let us be Your faithful servants today, tomorrow, and forever.

Amen.

More from God's Word

*Your old sinful self has died, and your new life
is kept with Christ in God.*

COLOSSIANS 3:3 NCV

*You are being renewed in the spirit of your minds; you
put on the new self, the one created according to God's
likeness in righteousness and purity of the truth.*

EPHESIANS 4:23–24 HCSB

*There is one thing I always do. Forgetting the past and
straining toward what is ahead, I keep trying to reach
the goal and get the prize for which God called me . . .*

PHILIPPIANS 3:13–14 NCV

*"For I know the plans I have for you"—this is the
LORD's declaration—"plans for your welfare,
not for disaster, to give you a future and a hope."*

JEREMIAH 29:11 HCSB

*The things which are impossible
with men are possible with God.*

LUKE 18:27 KJV

About New Beginnings

God is not running an antique shop!
He is making all things new!

VANCE HAVNER

There is wonderful freedom and joy in coming
to recognize that the fun is in the becoming.

GLORIA GAITHER

Faith does not concern itself with
the entire journey. One step is enough.

LETTIE COWMAN

The best preparation for the future is the present
well seen to, and the last duty done.

GEORGE MACDONALD

When we were baptized, we were buried with Christ
and shared his death. So, just as Christ was raised
from the dead by the wonderful power of the Father,
we also can live a new life.

ROMANS 6:4 NCV

42

Obedience

Obey Him

We must obey God rather than men.

ACTS 5:29 NASB

Dear Lord, You have promised to bless those who obey Your commandments. I ask that You lead me, Father, along a path of Your choosing. And I pray that my children will be Your obedient servants, now and forever.

I know, Lord, that Your commandments are a perfect guide for my family. Give us the wisdom to read Your Word, to discern Your will, and to follow in the footsteps of Your Son.

Your wisdom is a priceless gift. Let us listen, learn, and obey.

Amen.

More from God's Word

Teach me, O LORD, the way of Your statutes,
and I shall observe it to the end.

PSALM 119:33 NASB

Trust in the LORD with all your heart,
And lean not on your own understanding;
In all your ways acknowledge Him,
And He shall direct your paths.

PROVERBS 3:5–6 NKJV

Praise the LORD! Happy are those who respect the LORD,
who want what he commands.

PSALM 112:1 NCV

But prove yourselves doers of the word,
and not merely hearers who delude themselves.

JAMES 1:22 NASB

The highway of the upright avoids evil;
the one who guards his way protects his life.

PROVERBS 16:17 HCSB

About Obedience

The golden rule for understanding in spiritual matters
is not intellect, but obedience.

OSWALD CHAMBERS

When we are obedient,
God guides our steps and our stops.

CORRIE TEN BOOM

Obedience is the key to every door.

GEORGE MACDONALD

Obedience is the master key to effectual prayer.

BILLY GRAHAM

Happiness is obedience and obedience is happiness.

C. H. SPURGEON

Now by this we know that we know Him,
if we keep His commandments.

I JOHN 2:3 NKJV

43

Peace

He Promises Us Peace

*And the peace of God, which passeth
all understanding, shall keep your hearts
and minds through Christ Jesus.*

PHILIPPIANS 4:7 KJV

Dear Lord, You have promised that we can experience Your peace. Thank You, Father, for that priceless gift.

Today, I pray that my children will trust You, I pray that they will love You, and I pray that they will experience the peace that passes all understanding: Your peace. The peace that the world offers is fleeting, but You offer a peace that is perfect and eternal.

Let my family experience the spiritual abundance that You offer through Your Son, the Prince of Peace. We thank You, Father, for Your love, for Your peace, and for Your Son.

Amen.

More from God's Word

He Himself is our peace.

Ephesians 2:14 NASB

*But the fruit of the Spirit is love, joy, peace,
patience, kindness, goodness, faith, gentleness,
self-control. Against such things there is no law.*

Galatians 5:22–23 HCSB

*"I will give peace, real peace, to those far and near,
and I will heal them," says the* Lord.

Isaiah 57:19 NCV

*These things I have spoken to you, that in Me you may
have peace. In the world you will have tribulation;
but be of good cheer, I have overcome the world.*

John 16:33 NKJV

*The steadfast of mind You will keep
in perfect peace, because he trusts in You.*

Isaiah 26:3 NASB

About Peace

Deep within the center of the soul is a chamber
of peace where God lives and where,
if we will enter it and quiet all the other sounds,
we can hear His gentle whisper.

LETTIE COWMAN

What peace can they have who
are not at peace with God?

MATTHEW HENRY

God's peace is like a river, not a pond. In other words,
a sense of health and well-being, both of which are
expressions of the Hebrew shalom, *can permeate*
our homes even when we're in whitewater rapids.

BETH MOORE

Peace I leave with you, My peace I give to you;
not as the world gives do I give to you. Let not your
heart be troubled, neither let it be afraid.

JOHN 14:27 NKJV

44

Perseverance

The Power of Perseverance

Consider it pure joy, my brothers and sisters, whenever
you face trials of many kinds, because you know
that the testing of your faith develops perseverance.
Let perseverance finish its work so that you may
be mature and complete, not lacking anything.

JAMES 1:2–4 NIV

Heavenly Father, You have promised that when we persevere, we will be rewarded. But when we experience the inevitable hardships of life, we are sometimes tempted to abandon hope.

Dear Lord, I pray that my children learn to draw strength from You. Let them learn to persevere during life's darker days, so that they can earn the blessings that You have promised.

When our challenges seem insurmountable, let us remember that nothing is impossible for You, Father. When our strength is almost gone, we will depend upon You to renew our spirits and give us the courage to persevere.

Amen.

More from God's Word

But as for you, be strong; don't be discouraged,
for your work has a reward.

II Chronicles 15:7 HCSB

We are hard-pressed on every side, yet not crushed;
we are perplexed, but not in despair.

II Corinthians 4:8 NKJV

Finishing is better than starting.
Patience is better than pride.

Ecclesiastes 7:8 NLT

God is our refuge and strength, always ready to help
in times of trouble. So we will not fear when earthquakes
come and the mountains crumble into the sea.

Psalm 46:1–2 NLT

So let us run the race that is before us
and never give up. We should remove from
our lives anything that would get in the way
and the sin that so easily holds us back.

Hebrews 12:1 NCV

About Endurance and Perseverance

Perseverance is more than endurance. It is endurance
combined with absolute assurance and certainty
that what we are looking for is going to happen.

OSWALD CHAMBERS

Great accomplishments are often attempted but only
occasionally reached. Those who reach them are
usually those who have missed many times before.

CHARLES SWINDOLL

No amount of falls will really undo us if
we keep picking ourselves up after each one.

C. S. LEWIS

Everyone gets discouraged. The question is:
Are you going to give up or get up? It's a choice.

JOHN MAXWELL

Let us not become weary in doing good,
for at the proper time we will reap
a harvest if we do not give up.

GALATIANS 6:9 NIV

45

Praise

Praise Him

Great is the LORD! He is most worthy of praise!
No one can measure his greatness.

PSALM 145:3 NLT

Dear Lord, I praise You for the countless blessings You have bestowed upon myself and my family. Today, I pray that my children will praise You with a song on their lips and a prayer in their hearts.

Heavenly Father, this is the day that You have made. Let us rejoice; let us be grateful; and let us offer praise for gifts that are simply too numerous to count.

Great is Your faithfulness, Lord. Let our praise also be great now and forever.

Amen.

More from God's Word

In everything give thanks; for this is the will
of God in Christ Jesus for you.

I Thessalonians 5:18 NKJV

At the name of Jesus every knee should bow, of things
in heaven, and things in earth, and things under the
earth; and that every tongue should confess that Jesus
Christ is Lord, to the glory of God the Father.

Philippians 2:10–11 KJV

The Lord is my strength and my song;
He has become my salvation.

Exodus 15:2 HCSB

From the rising of the sun to its setting
The name of the Lord is to be praised.

Psalm 113:3 NASB

I will praise you, Lord, with all my heart.
I will tell all the miracles you have done.
I will be happy because of you;
God Most High, I will sing praises to your name.

Psalm 9:1–2 NCV

About Praise

Two wings are necessary to lift our souls
toward God: prayer and praise.
Prayer asks. Praise accepts the answer.

LETTIE COWMAN

Praising God reduces your cares,
levels your anxieties,
and multiplies your blessings.

SUZANNE DALE EZELL

Preoccupy my thoughts with
your praise beginning today.

JONI EARECKSON TADA

The time for universal praise is sure
to come some day. Let us begin to do our part now.

HANNAH WHITALL SMITH

Let everything that breathes
praise the LORD. Hallelujah!

PSALM 150:6 HCSB

46

Prayer

The Promise of Answered Prayer

*Ask, and it will be given to you; seek,
and you will find; knock, and it will be opened to you.
For everyone who asks receives, and he who seeks
finds, and to him who knocks it will be opened.*

MATTHEW 7:7–8 NASB

Heavenly Father, I thank You for hearing my prayers. You have promised that You are with me always. I pray that my children will talk to You often and listen carefully to Your responses.

Today, Father, we will ask You for the things we need. When we have concerns, we will take them to You. When we have fears, we will be mindful of Your love and Your protection. When we endure hardships, we will open our hearts to You. In matters great and small, we will seek Your guidance, and we will trust the answers that You give today and every day.

Amen.

More from God's Word

I desire therefore that the men pray everywhere,
lifting up holy hands, without wrath and doubting.

I Timothy 2:8 NKJV

Is anyone among you suffering? He should pray.

James 5:13 HCSB

Confess your trespasses to one another, and pray
for one another, that you may be healed. The effective,
fervent prayer of a righteous man avails much.

James 5:16 NKJV

And whenever you stand praying, if you have anything
against anyone, forgive him, so that your Father
in heaven will also forgive you your wrongdoing.

Mark 11:25 HCSB

"I prayed for this child, and the Lord has granted me
what I asked of him. So now I give him to the Lord.
For his whole life he will be given over to the Lord."

I Samuel 1:27–28 NIV

About the Power of Prayer

Prayer is our lifeline to God.

BILLY GRAHAM

You must go forward on your knees.

HUDSON TAYLOR

Is prayer your steering wheel or your spare tire?

CORRIE TEN BOOM

Two wings are necessary to lift our souls toward God:
prayer and praise. Prayer asks.
Praise accepts the answer.

LETTIE COWMAN

Don't pray when you feel like it.
Have an appointment with the Lord and keep it.

CORRIE TEN BOOM

Rejoice always, pray without ceasing,
in everything give thanks;
for this is the will of God in Christ Jesus for you.

I THESSALONIANS 5:16–18 NKJV

47

Purpose

Finding Meaning and Purpose

You will show me the path of life;
in Your presence is fullness of joy;
at Your right hand are pleasures forevermore.

PSALM 16:11 NKJV

Dear Lord, You have promised to show us the path of life, and I pray that my children will seek Your guidance and follow Your instructions for life here on earth and for life eternal.

Father, You are the Creator of the universe, and I know that Your plans for my family are grander than I can imagine. Thank You, Father, for Your gifts.

Let Your purposes be our purposes, Lord, and let us trust in the assurance of Your promises today and every day of our lives.

Amen.

More from God's Word

For we are God's coworkers.
You are God's field, God's building.

I Corinthians 3:9 HCSB

For we are His creation, created in Christ Jesus
for good works, which God prepared
ahead of time so that we should walk in them.

Ephesians 2:10 HCSB

We must do the works of Him who sent Me
while it is day. Night is coming when no one can work.

John 9:4 HCSB

So whether you eat or drink, or whatever you do,
do it all for the glory of God.

I Corinthians 10:31 NLT

And whatever you do, do it heartily,
as to the Lord and not to men.

Colossians 3:23 NKJV

About Meaning and Purpose

The easiest way to discover the purpose
of an invention is to ask the creator of it. The same
is true for discovering your life's purpose: ask God.

RICK WARREN

You weren't an accident. You weren't mass-produced.
You aren't an assembly-line product. You were
deliberately planned, specifically gifted, and lovingly
positioned on the Earth by the Master Craftsman.

MAX LUCADO

There's some task which the God of all the universe,
the great Creator, has for you to do, and which will
remain undone and incomplete, until by faith
and obedience, you step into the will of God.

ALAN REDPATH

We have also received an inheritance in Him,
predestined according to the purpose
of the One who works out everything
in agreement with the decision of His will.

EPHESIANS 1:11 HCSB

48

Renewal

The Promise of Renewal

Those who hope in the Lord will renew their strength.
They will soar on wings like eagles; they will run
and not grow weary, they will walk and not be faint.

Isaiah 40:31 NIV

Heavenly Father, You have promised to renew our spirits and restore our strength. Today, I pray that my children will trust that You, and You alone, are the Rock upon which they must build their lives.

When they endure difficult days, I pray that my children will turn to You for strength, Lord. And if they lose their bearings, give them a fresh start and a new heart—a heart that reflects Your love.

Whenever we need to change, Lord, give us the wisdom to seek Your guidance and the courage to follow Your lead.

Amen.

More from God's Word

You are being renewed in the spirit of your minds; you put on the new self, the one created according to God's likeness in righteousness and purity of the truth.

EPHESIANS 4:23–24 HCSB

Remember ye not the former things, neither consider the things of old. Behold, I will do a new thing . . .

ISAIAH 43:18–19 KJV

Finally, brothers, rejoice. Become mature, be encouraged, be of the same mind, be at peace, and the God of love and peace will be with you.

II CORINTHIANS 13:11 HCSB

Now the God of all grace, who called you to His eternal glory in Christ Jesus, will personally restore, establish, strengthen, and support you . . .

I PETER 5:10 HCSB

I lift up my eyes to the mountains—where does my help come from? My help comes from the LORD, the Maker of heaven and earth.

PSALM 121:1–2 NIV

About Renewal

God specializes in giving people a fresh start.

RICK WARREN

*The truth is, God's strength is fully revealed
when our strength is depleted.*

LIZ CURTIS HIGGS

*The creation of a new heart, the renewing
of a right spirit is an omnipotent work of God.
Leave it to the Creator.*

HENRY DRUMMOND

*Are you weak? Weary? Confused? Troubled? Pressured?
How is your relationship with God? Is it held in its
place of priority? I believe the greater the pressure,
the greater your need for time alone with Him.*

KAY ARTHUR

*Therefore, if anyone is in Christ,
he is a new creation; old things have passed away;
behold, all things have become new.*

II CORINTHIANS 5:17 NKJV

49

Righteousness

He Instructs Us to Be Righteous

*Sow righteousness for yourselves, reap the fruit
of unfailing love, and break up your unplowed ground;
for it is time to seek the LORD, until he comes
and showers righteousness on you.*

HOSEA 10:12 NIV

Dear Lord, I pray that my children will live righteously. I pray that they will be trustworthy and obedient to the teachings they find in Your holy Word.

This world is brimming with countless temptations, distractions, and dangers of every kind. I pray that my children can avoid these traps.

I ask that You help every member of my family discern Your will and fulfill the responsibilities that You have placed before us. Give us the wisdom to understand Your will for our lives, and give us the strength to meet the challenges of everyday life. Let us open our hearts to You today, tomorrow, and forever.

Amen.

More from God's Word

Discipline yourself for the purpose of godliness.

I TIMOTHY 4:7 NASB

And let us not grow weary while doing good,
for in due season we shall reap if we do not lose heart.

GALATIANS 6:9 NKJV

But godliness with contentment is a great gain.

I TIMOTHY 6:6 HCSB

Now by this we know that we know Him,
if we keep His commandments.

I JOHN 2:3 NKJV

For the eyes of the Lord are over the righteous,
and his ears are open unto their prayers:
but the face of the Lord is against them that do evil.

I PETER 3:12 KJV

About Righteousness and Goodness

We have two natures within us, both struggling
for mastery. Which one will dominate us?
It depends on which one we feed.

BILLY GRAHAM

Give to us clear vision that we may know where
to stand and what to stand for—because unless we
stand for something, we shall fall for anything.

PETER MARSHALL

I believe that in every time and place it is within
our power to acquiesce in the will of God—
and what peace it brings to do so!

ELISABETH ELLIOT

Never support an experience which does not have God
as its source and faith in God as its result.

OSWALD CHAMBERS

The result of righteousness will be peace; the effect
of righteousness will be quiet confidence forever.

ISAIAH 32:17 HCSB

50

Salvation

The Promise of Salvation

For God so loved the world, that he gave his only begotten Son, that whosoever believeth in him should not perish, but have everlasting life.

JOHN 3:16 KJV

Heavenly Father, You have offered me the priceless gift of eternal life through Your Son. I have accepted Your gift, Lord, with thanksgiving and praise. Now I pray that my children will accept the gift of salvation through Jesus.

Because we are mere mortals with limited vision and limited experiences, we cannot fully comprehend the glories of heaven. But You can. And You know the joys that await us there.

I ask that You help my children understand the critical need to accept Jesus as their Savior. When we become Christ's disciples, and when we follow closely in His footsteps, we will be blessed, now and forever.

Amen.

More from God's Word

And we have seen and testify that the Father
has sent the Son as Savior of the world.

I JOHN 4:14 NKJV

Jesus said to her, "I am the resurrection and the life.
The one who believes in me will live,
even though they die; and whoever lives
by believing in me will never die."

JOHN 11:25–26 NIV

I tell you the truth,
anyone who believes has eternal life.

JOHN 6:47 NLT

Sing to the LORD, all the earth;
proclaim his salvation day after day.

I CHRONICLES 16:23 NIV

The LORD is my strength and my song;
He has become my salvation.

EXODUS 15:2 HCSB

About Salvation

Salvation comes through a cross and a crucified Christ.

ANDREW MURRAY

God is not saving the world; it is done.
Our business is to get men and women to realize it.

OSWALD CHAMBERS

Christ not only died for all: He died for each.

BILLY GRAHAM

Christ is the horn of our salvation,
the One who was secured on a cross so that we
could be secured in the Lamb's Book of Life.

BETH MOORE

He saved us, not on the basis of deeds
which we have done in righteousness,
but according to His mercy, by the washing
of regeneration and renewing by the Holy Spirit.

TITUS 3:5 NASB

51

Satan

Victory over Satan

Be sober, be vigilant; because your adversary
the devil walks about like a roaring lion,
seeking whom he may devour.

I Peter 5:8 NKJV

Dear Lord, You know that our enemy, Satan, is constantly seeking to destroy us. All of us, parents and children alike, are vulnerable to the devil's temptations.

Today, I ask you for the wisdom to see Satan's traps and the courage to avoid them. And I pray that my children will be watchful and strong as they, too, resist the enemy's deceptions.

Satan is constantly at work, attempting to influence our thoughts and our actions. I ask that You give my family the strength and the wisdom to overcome the enemy by committing ourselves to Your Word, to Your will, and to Your Son.

Amen.

More from God's Word

Put on the full armor of God so that you can stand against the tactics of the Devil.

Ephesians 6:11 HCSB

Therefore submit to God. Resist the devil and he will flee from you. Draw near to God and He will draw near to you. Cleanse your hands, you sinners; and purify your hearts, you double-minded.

James 4:7–8 NKJV

Don't fear those who kill the body but are not able to kill the soul; rather, fear Him who is able to destroy both soul and body in hell.

Matthew 10:28 HCSB

Dear friend, do not imitate what is evil, but what is good. The one who does good is of God; the one who does evil has not seen God.

III John 1:11 HCSB

About Victory over the Enemy

Measure your growth in grace
by your sensitivity to sin.

OSWALD CHAMBERS

There are two great forces at work
in the world today: the unlimited power of God
and the limited power of Satan.

CORRIE TEN BOOM

Of two evils, choose neither.

C. H. SPURGEON

Just as courage is faith in good, so discouragement
is faith in evil, and, while courage opens the door
to good, discouragement opens it to evil.

HANNAH WHITALL SMITH

Be strong! We must prove ourselves strong
for our people and for the cities of our God.
May the LORD's will be done.

I CHRONICLES 19:13 HCSB

52

Spiritual Blessings

He Blesses the Righteous

*For You, LORD, bless the righteous one;
You surround him with favor like a shield.*

PSALM 5:12 HCSB

Heavenly Father, You have promised to bless the righteous. I pray that my children will live righteously and receive the spiritual blessings that You reserve for those who study Your Word and obey the commandments they find there.

You, Father, are the Giver of all good gifts. And I praise You for the blessings You have bestowed upon my family and myself. I give thanks for Your creation, for Your Son, and for the unique talents and opportunities that You have given my children. Give them the wisdom and the courage to use their gifts for the glory of Your kingdom, this day and every day.

Amen.

More from God's Word

*I will make them and the places surrounding
my hill a blessing. I will send down showers
in season; there will be showers of blessing.*

Ezekiel 34:26 NIV

*For the LORD watches over the way of the righteous,
but the way of the wicked leads to ruin.*

Psalm 1:6 HCSB

*Don't be afraid, because I am your God.
I will make you strong and will help you; I will
support you with my right hand that saves you.*

Isaiah 41:10 NCV

*Know the love of Christ which surpasses knowledge,
that you may be filled up to all the fullness of God.*

Ephesians 3:19 NASB

*The LORD bless you and keep you;
The LORD make His face shine upon you,
And be gracious to you.*

Numbers 6:24–25 NKJV

About Spiritual Blessings

*The gift of God is eternal life, spiritual life,
abundant life through faith in Jesus Christ,
the Living Word of God.*

ANNE GRAHAM LOTZ

*Spiritual maturity is becoming more
and more like Christ, and if you make
this your goal, it will change your life.*

BILLY GRAHAM

*The vigor of our spiritual life will be
in exact proportion to the place held
by the Bible in our life and thoughts.*

GEORGE MÜLLER

*Joy is the direct result of having God's perspective
on our daily lives and the effect of loving our Lord
enough to obey His commands and trust His promises.*

BILL BRIGHT

Blessings are on the head of the righteous.

PROVERBS 10:6 HCSB

53

Spiritual Growth

The Path to Spiritual Growth

*But grow in the grace and knowledge of our Lord
and Savior Jesus Christ. To Him be the glory
both now and forever. Amen.*

II Peter 3:18 NKJV

Dear Lord, I pray that my children will continue to grow spiritually and emotionally today and every day of their lives.

Father, You know that my children are citizens of a dangerous society; They inhabit a world in which the enemy is constantly searching for someone to destroy. Protect my children, Lord, and let them grow in the grace and knowledge of the Lord and Savior, Jesus Christ.

I thank You, Lord, for my children, and I pray that they will live each day with praise on their lips and love in their hearts.

Amen.

More from God's Word

But endurance must do its complete work, so that you may be mature and complete, lacking nothing.

And be not conformed to this world: but be ye transformed by the renewing of your mind, that ye may prove what is that good, and acceptable, and perfect, will of God.

ROMANS 12:2 KJV

So let us stop going over the basic teachings about Christ again and again. Let us go on instead and become mature in our understanding.

HEBREWS 6:1 NLT

Teach me your ways, O LORD, that I may live according to your truth! Grant me purity of heart, so that I may honor you.

PSALM 86:11 NLT

About Spiritual Growth

Grow, dear friends, but grow, I beseech you,
in God's way, which is the only true way.

Hannah Whitall Smith

Spiritual growth doesn't happen automatically
and is rarely pretty; we will all be "under construction"
until the day we die and we finally take hold of the
"life that is truly life" (I Tim. 6:19).

Kay Warren

We look at our burdens and heavy loads,
and we shrink from them. But if we lift them and bind
them about our hearts, they become wings,
and on them we can rise and soar toward God.

Lettie Cowman

Mark it down. You will never go where God is not.

Max Lucado

I remind you to fan into flames
the spiritual gift God gave you . . .

II Timothy 1:6 NLT

54

Strength

The Promise of Strength

*The L*ORD *is my strength and my song;*
He has become my salvation.

EXODUS 15:2 HCSB

Dear Lord, You promise to give us the strength we need to accomplish Your purposes. I pray that my children will trust Your promises and claim Your strength.

Heavenly Father, I pray that every member of my family will turn to You for strength. When our responsibilities seem overwhelming, I pray that we will trust You to give us courage and perspective.

You have promised that You will provide for our needs, Lord. Let us trust in the perfect wisdom of Your plan. Today, let us look to You as the ultimate Source of strength, hope, and peace.

Amen.

More from God's Word

My grace is sufficient for you,
for my power is made perfect in weakness.

II Corinthians 12:9 NIV

Have faith in the Lord your God,
and you will stand strong. Have faith in his prophets,
and you will succeed.

II Chronicles 20:20 NCV

Be of good courage, and he shall strengthen
your heart, all ye that hope in the Lord.

Psalm 31:24 KJV

Be strong and courageous, and do the work.
Don't be afraid or discouraged,
for the Lord God, my God, is with you.
He won't leave you or forsake you. . . .

I Chronicles 28:20 HCSB

I can do all things through Christ who strengthens me.

Philippians 4:13 NKJV

About Strength

Faith is a strong power,
mastering any difficulty in the strength
of the Lord who made heaven and earth.

Corrie ten Boom

Refuse to waste energy worrying,
and you will have strength to spare.

Sarah Young

Strength is found not in busyness
and noise but in quietness.

Lettie Cowman

The truth is, God's strength is fully revealed
when our strength is depleted.

Liz Curtis Higgs

He gives strength to the weary,
and to him who lacks might He increases power.

Isaiah 40:29 NASB

55

Success

He Promises to Direct Our Steps

Trust in the LORD with all your heart,
And lean not on your own understanding;
In all your ways acknowledge Him,
And He shall direct your paths.

<small>PROVERBS 3:5–6 NKJV</small>

Dear Lord, I pray that my children will honor You with their thoughts, their prayers, and their actions. And I pray that You will guide them through every phase of life. You are their Shepherd, Lord, and I thank You for Your guidance and protection.

The world defines success in material terms, but You, Father, know that genuine success is a matter of the heart, not the pocketbook.

I pray that my children will learn what true success is, and what it isn't. And I pray that they will use Your Word as their guidebook for life here on earth and for life eternal.

Amen.

More from God's Word

There is no wisdom, understanding,
or advice that can succeed against the LORD.

PROVERBS 21:30 NCV

Those who work their land will have abundant food,
but those who chase fantasies have no sense.

PROVERBS 12:11 NIV

Good comes to those who lend money generously
and conduct their business fairly.

PSALM 112:5 NLT

Who are those who fear the LORD?
He will show them the path they should choose.
They will live in prosperity,
and their children will inherit the land.

PSALM 25:12–13 NLT

But as it is written: "Eye has not seen, nor ear heard,
nor have entered into the heart of man the things
which God has prepared for those who love Him."

I CORINTHIANS 2:9 NKJV

About Success

Every difficult task that comes across your path—
every one that you would rather not do,
that will take the most effort, cause the most pain,
and be the greatest struggle—brings a blessing with it.

LETTIE COWMAN

If you're running a 26-mile marathon, remember that
every mile is run one step at a time. There are 365
days in the average year. Divide any project by 365
and you'll find that no job is all that intimidating.

CHARLES SWINDOLL

True greatness is found in someone's soul,
not in his social standing or position.

SAINT THÉRÈSE OF LISIEUX

May he give you the desire of your heart
and make all your plans succeed.

PSALM 20:4 NIV

56

Temptation

He Promises to Protect Us from Temptation

Put on the whole armor of God, that you may be able to stand against the wiles of the devil.

Ephesians 6:11 NKJV

Dear Lord, You know that we live in a world that is filled with temptations and distractions. And you know that the enemy is constantly at work, trying to deceive us, trying to distract us, and, ultimately, trying to destroy us. Protect us from the enemy, Father, and from the temptations that he uses to cause us harm.

I pray that my children will be wise enough and strong enough to resist Satan's ploys. And I pray that they will never yield to the temptations of this dangerous world.

I ask that You guide my children, Lord, and that You keep them mindful of Your truth, Your wisdom, and Your love.

Amen.

More from God's Word

No temptation has overtaken you
but such as is common to man; and God is faithful,
who will not allow you to be tempted
beyond what you are able, but with the temptation
will provide the way of escape . . .

I Corinthians 10:13 NASB

Do not be misled: "Bad company
corrupts good character."

I Corinthians 15:33 NIV

Let us lay aside every weight,
and the sin which so easily ensnares us,
and let us run with endurance
the race that is set before us.

Hebrews 12:1 NKJV

A man who endures trials is blessed, because when
he passes the test he will receive the crown of life
that God has promised to those who love Him.

James 1:12 HCSB

About Temptation

Temptations that have been anticipated,
guarded against, and prayed about have little power
to harm us. Jesus tells us to "keep watching
and praying, that you may not come into temptation."

JOHN MACARTHUR

The first step on the way to victory
is to recognize the enemy.

CORRIE TEN BOOM

It is not the temptations you have, but the decision
you make about them, that counts.

BILLY GRAHAM

Every temptation, directly or indirectly,
is the temptation to doubt and distrust God.

JOHN MACARTHUR

Your adversary, the devil, prowls around
like a roaring lion, seeking someone to devour.

I PETER 5:8 NASB

57

Thanksgiving

Thankful for His Blessings

And whatever you do, in word or in deed,
do everything in the name of the Lord Jesus,
giving thanks to God the Father through Him.

Colossians 3:17 HCSB

Heavenly Father, You have blessed my family in so many ways. I pray that we will be appropriately grateful for Your gifts. And I pray that my children will praise You for their blessings.

Father, I know that all good gifts come from You. I pray that my children will understand that every gift and every opportunity is a gift from above.

Dear Lord, You are generous and kind. You are merciful and loving. You protect us and You bless us every day of our lives. May we be thankful today, tomorrow, and forever.

Amen.

More from God's Word

Rejoice always, pray without ceasing,
in everything give thanks;
for this is the will of God in Christ Jesus for you.

I Thessalonians 5:16–18 NKJV

Surely the righteous shall give thanks to Your name;
The upright shall dwell in Your presence.

Psalm 140:13 NKJV

I will thank Yahweh with all my heart;
I will declare all Your wonderful works.
I will rejoice and boast about You;
I will sing about Your name, Most High.

Psalm 9:1–2 HCSB

Thanks be to God for His indescribable gift.

II Corinthians 9:15 HCSB

About Thanksgiving

*If you can't tell whether your glass is half-empty
or half-full, you don't need another glass; what you
need is better eyesight . . . and a more thankful heart.*

MARIE T. FREEMAN

*Why should we give God thanks?
Because everything we have comes from God.*

BILLY GRAHAM

*Thanksgiving will draw our hearts out to God
and keep us engaged with Him.*

ANDREW MURRAY

*Enter into His gates with thanksgiving,
And into His courts with praise.
Be thankful to Him, and bless His name.
For the LORD is good;
His mercy is everlasting,
And His truth endures to all generations.*

PSALM 100:4–5 NKJV

58

Trusting God

God Promises
That We Can Trust Him

Those who trust in the LORD are like Mount Zion.
It cannot be shaken; it remains forever.

PSALM 125:1 HCSB

Dear Lord, You are the Shepherd, and we are the sheep of Your pasture. I pray that my children will trust You to guide them and protect them through every circumstance and through every stage of life.

When my children are anxious, I pray that they will turn all of their worries, all of their anxieties, and all of their concerns over to You. I pray that they will trust Your wisdom, Your plan, Your promises, and Your Son.

Ultimately, I know that my children are in Your hands, Father. I thank You for Your care, for Your protection, and for Your love.

Amen.

More from God's Word

In quietness and trust is your strength.

Isaiah 30:15 NASB

The LORD is my rock, my fortress,
and my deliverer, my God,
my mountain where I seek refuge.
My shield, the horn of my salvation,
my stronghold, my refuge, and my Savior . . .

II Samuel 22:2–3 HCSB

The fear of man is a snare,
but the one who trusts in the LORD is protected.

Proverbs 29:25 HCSB

Jesus said, "Don't let your hearts be troubled.
Trust in God, and trust in me."

John 14:1 NCV

About Trusting God

*One of the marks of spiritual maturity is the quiet
confidence that God is in control, without the need
to understand why he does what he does.*

CHARLES SWINDOLL

*When trust is perfect and there is no doubt,
prayer is simply the outstretched hand ready to receive.*

E. M. BOUNDS

*Never yield to gloomy anticipation. Place your hope
and confidence in God. He has no record of failure.*

LETTIE COWMAN

*Trusting in Jesus Christ has changed me so completely
that I scarcely know my former self.*

C. H. SPURGEON

*Trust in the LORD with all your heart,
And lean not on your own understanding;
In all your ways acknowledge Him,
And He shall direct your paths.*

PROVERBS 3:5–6 NKJV

59

Understanding

Understanding and Wisdom

For this reason also, since the day we heard this,
we haven't stopped praying for you. We are asking
that you may be filled with the knowledge of His will
in all wisdom and spiritual understanding.

COLOSSIANS 1:9 HCSB

Dear Lord, the Bible instructs all of Your children to acquire wisdom. And I know that the ultimate wisdom is found on the pages of Your holy Word. So I will study Your teachings and do my best to honor You with clear thoughts, with sincere prayers, and with an obedient heart. And I pray that my children will look to You as their Source of wisdom and spiritual understanding. I ask that You guide them, Father, every day of their lives.

I pray that every member of my family will seek Your wisdom and live by it. When we trust in the wisdom of the world, we are often led astray, but when we trust You, Lord, we build our lives upon a firm foundation. Let us trust in You now and forever.

Amen.

More from God's Word

*A foolish person enjoys doing wrong, but a person
with understanding enjoys doing what is wise.*

PROVERBS 10:23 NCV

*A wise man will hear, and will
increase learning; and a man of understanding
shall attain unto wise counsels . . .*

PROVERBS 1:5 KJV

*Wisdom and strength belong to God;
counsel and understanding are His.*

JOB 12:13 HCSB

*Who among you is wise and understanding?
Let him show by his good behavior
his deeds in the gentleness of wisdom.*

JAMES 3:13 NASB

*Buy the truth, and do not sell it,
Also wisdom and instruction and understanding.*

PROVERBS 23:23 NKJV

About Understanding and Wisdom

God will see to it that we understand
as much truth as we are willing to obey.

ELISABETH ELLIOT

It is only by obedience that we understand
the teaching of God.

OSWALD CHAMBERS

If you lack knowledge, go to school.
If you lack wisdom, get on your knees!

VANCE HAVNER

If we neglect the Bible, we cannot expect
to benefit from the wisdom and direction that
result from knowing God's Word.

VONETTE BRIGHT

Morning by morning he wakens me
and opens my understanding to his will. The Sovereign
LORD has spoken to me, and I have listened. . . .

ISAIAH 50:4–5 NLT

60

Worship

He Instructs Us to Worship Him

Happy are those who hear the joyful call to worship,
for they will walk in the light of your presence, LORD.

PSALM 89:15 NLT

Dear Lord, I pray that my children will worship You with joy in their hearts and praise on their lips. You have blessed my children in so many ways. I pray that they will express their gratitude and acknowledge Your grace through praise and worship.

Heavenly Father, You are the Way, the Truth, and the Light. I pray that You will be a light to my entire family.

Today, as we follow in the footsteps of Your Son and share His good news with the world, let us worship Him in Spirit and in truth. May we be worthy examples to the people we meet along the way and worthy servants to You.

Amen.

More from God's Word

All the earth will worship You and sing praise to You.
They will sing praise to Your name.

PSALM 66:4 HCSB

God is Spirit, and those who worship Him
must worship in spirit and truth.

JOHN 4:24 HCSB

For where two or three are gathered together
in My name, I am there among them.

MATTHEW 18:20 HCSB

Worship the LORD with gladness.
Come before him, singing with joy.
Acknowledge that the LORD is God!
He made us, and we are his.
We are his people, the sheep of his pasture.

PSALM 100:2–3 NLT

About Worship

Worship is an inward reverence, the bowing down of the soul in the presence of God.

ELIZABETH GEORGE

We must worship in truth. Worship is not just an emotional exercise but a response of the heart built on truth about God.

ERWIN LUTZER

Learn to shut out the distractions that keep you from truly worshiping God.

BILLY GRAHAM

Worship in the truest sense takes place only when our full attention is on God— His glory, majesty, love, and compassion.

BILLY GRAHAM

I was glad when they said unto me, Let us go into the house of the LORD.

PSALM 122:1 KJV